NASA National Aeronautics and Space Administration

Harry M. Meyer, Jr., M.D.

William B. Catton

W9-AOR-881

HARVARD UNIVERSITY

YORTY

arbor Laboratory

STOCKHOLMS UNIVERSITET

L. RON HUBBARD

DANNY THOMAS

D. Watson
rector

JOSHUA LOGA

The Institute For Psychoanalysis

Barry Goldwater

Bayard Rustin

ZBIGNIEW BRZEZINSKI

Dean Rusk

oreland

Retired

th best wishes from West Point

Hal Wallis

MARY KAY

A. J. GOODPASTER
Lt. General, U.S. Army

MICKEY SPILLANE

OCHSNER CLINIC

Deborah Kerr Viertel

Morris K.

Yehudi Menuhin

TEMPLE SINAI

MELVIN BELLI

Romero

Liz Smith
Syndicated Columnist
New York Daily News

STATE SENATOR JULIAN BOND

Al Worden

Brigham and Women's Hospital

Margaret Chase Smith

JAMES ROOSEVELT

OFFICE OF

GERALD R. FORD

Cabinet du Roi

Joseph T. English, M.D.

A. Greenwalt

ND WILDLIFE SERVICE

Chancellor, University of Moratuwa

MICHAEL CRICHTON

Arthur C Clarke

San Francisco Symphony Association

rty Bowl Football Classic

DR. JAMES DEWEY WATSON

HE PRESIDENT IS SWORN IN

Isabel Sanford

ITALIAN CULTURAL INSTITUTE

CIATES

SARAH T. HUGHES
nited States District Judge

PONTIFICIA COMMISSIONE PER LE COMUNICAZIONI SOCIALI

Albert Speer
German armaments mini

The Star

JOHN (JOHNNY) GREEN

NOVEMBER 22, 1963

City of Birmingham,
OFFICE OF THE MAYOR
February 1, 1984

die Elliott Hansen
al
City, TN 38261

Mrs. Hansen:

I thank you for allowing me the opportunity to share with you some details of what I was doing and my initial reaction to the death of President John F. Kennedy.

I was in attendance at a statewide science program at the University of Oklahoma in Norman. As I walked into the room where the seminar was being held, I realized that a number of students were viewing a television set with such attention. In an effort to determine what has so completely captured their attention, I went forward only to discover the awful truth. The young President, who many of us in this nation and the world viewed with so much admiration, had been slain.

I was deeply saddened as I was optimistic that Mr. Kennedy's administration would get the nation moving in the right direction. Indeed, he had inspired us all. He had given us hope. He had shared a vision, with all America that was at once idealistic but at the same time pragmatic. Certainly as a black person, I had dreams that with Mr. Kennedy's election we could now look to the White House to right many of the wrongs that I felt were unjustly visited upon blacks all over this land. But now this dream was all over; it had degenerated into a nightmare!

I was stunned and angered. My first reaction was to apportion blame, but I quickly discovered that I knew of no one to fault for this tragedy. I experienced a feeling of emptiness, of hurt that was beyond measure. Mercifully, as time wore on, this feeling of quiet anger and sadness began to subside but not disappear. To this very day, "That day in Dallas" troubles me whenever I think of what might have been had Mr. Kennedy lived to implement his policies which I firmly supported.

Sincerely,

Richard Arrington Jr.

Richard Arrington, Jr.
Mayor

RA/wf

March 19, 1980

Mrs. Jodie Elliott Hansen
Box 1031
Union City, Tennessee 38261

Dear Mrs. Hansen:

Your letter regarding your book was received just last week. Thus the delay in responding.

To the best of my recollection, this was what took place in my that sad, eventful day in history, 1962.

At the time, I was a coach for the Houston Oilers of the American League. At the conclusion of practice, someone broke the news President, John F. Kennedy, had been shot in Dallas, Texas. was hard to accept and immediately began to pray for his life A friend of mine, another coach, and I, showered, dressed a drive through congested traffic, homeward. We, with thous the Houston area, continued to listen via radio to the progress. Still in a state of disbelief, I thought back time, to the assassination of another President, Abra other such event had taken place in my lifetime was un

office of the President of the United States is, w respected by me as one of greatness in every way. that filled this office with dignity and to see a memory, was tragic, and this country will fore ch.

that the office of the President of the Unit experience such an event.

re the things that I remember on that day

re best wishes to you.

Sincerely you

Neill

Neill Arms
Head Coach

HARRISON STREET
NEW YORK, N.Y. 10013

Dear Mrs. Hansen;

Your letter of March 8th **did** arrive, and I only now on my return from a long travel.

To reply to your question; I was in Odessa, U.S. a cultural exchange visit (John Steinbeck and I going together) and I --plus my U.S. Embassy escort, William later U.S. Ambassador to Venezuela -- had just been to there for a dreadful production of a minor Rimsky-Korsako opera. We walked back from the opera house to the hotel, o menting on the peculiar strident quality of so many Russian ranos. When we entered the hotel we were startled to hear the Voice of America (unjammed) announcing the shooting and death of Kennedy. The lobby, and the great stairs of the hotel, were filled with disbelieving and weeping people --U.S. and other. I recall being more homesick and lonely than ever before or since in my life.

Regards,

Edward Albee

City of L[os Angeles]

CITY HALL
LOS ANGELES, CALIFORNIA 90012
(213) 485-3311

OFFICE OF THE

August 3,

Mrs. Jodie Elliott Hansen
Box 1031
Union City, Tennessee 38261

Dear Mrs. Hansen:

n response to your letter requesting informat as doing at the time I first heard the news o f President John F. Kennedy, I am sending the

was attending a City Council meeting; and one e Council, Mrs. Rosalyn Wyman, came back from nounced over the loudspeaker in the Council Ch esident Kennedy had been shot in Dallas. We al ence for several seconds and then a motion was ourn the Council meeting.

uickly returned to my office to get direct radi firm the gravity of the situation. There was a ch pervaded the entire City Hall and hardly any rred between people. I felt a sense of emptine h had been unmatched in my lifetime. I later w simply drove around the streets of Los Angeles f our. During that drive, I observed the look of aces of everyone and witnessed an unreal quietne City. Never have I felt such a sense of loss. T ng will remain etched in my mind forever.

Very truly yours,

Tom Bradley

TOM BRADLEY
MAYOR

So many americans from Photographer Cecil Shough the President himself to the occasion and left this country to **continuity** I drafted the words he on arriving in Washington but really had drafted them. Some greater Car saw us all Athens --

Fox Carpenter

I believe Broadway was dark for several nights — I'm not certain how many performances we cancelled.

I am sure your book will be most interesting — All my best wishes

Carlotta Col[e]

Monday 29 June —

NOVEMBER 22, 1963

━⊶⫸⟋⫷⊷━

Ordinary and Extraordinary People Recall Their Reactions When They Heard the News

JODIE ELLIOTT HANSEN

AND

LAURA HANSEN

THOMAS DUNNE BOOKS · ST. MARTIN'S PRESS ✠ NEW YORK

THOMAS DUNNE BOOKS.
An imprint of St. Martin's Press.

NOVEMBER 22, 1963. Copyright © 2013 by Jodie Elliott Hansen and Laura Hansen. All rights reserved. Printed in the United States of America. For information, address St. Martin's Press, 175 Fifth Avenue, New York, N.Y. 10010.

www.thomasdunnebooks.com
www.stmartins.com

DESIGN BY CLAIRE NAYLON VACCARO
Production manager: Lisa Viviani Goris
Production editor: Eric C. Meyer

Library of Congress Cataloging-in-Publication Data

Hansen, Jodie Elliott.
  November 22, 1963 : ordinary and extraordinary people recall their reactions when they heard the news / compiled by Jodie Elliott Hansen ; edited by Laura Hansen.
    pages cm
  ISBN 978-1-250-03748-0 (hardcover)
  ISBN 978-1-250-03747-3 (e-book)
1. Kennedy, John F. (John Fitzgerald), 1917-1963—Assassination. I. Hansen, Laura. II. Title.
  E842.9.H273 2013
  973.922092—dc23   2013026715

First Edition: November 2013

10 9 8 7 6 5 4 3 2 1

To my eleven perfect grandchildren: Gordon, Catey Laura,

Hannah, Mary Catherine, Grady, Finn, Kevin, Cal,

Christopher, Kensington, and Ricky. I thank you for the

many years of joyful sounds and the wonderful memories, as

each one of you discovered and explored this world with an

innocent curiosity and a wide-eyed sense of wonder.

INTRODUCTION

It takes a thousand voices to tell a single story.

In 1978 my mother, Jodie Hansen, was researching her family history and came across a small news item about her relatives in an 1865 newspaper filled with reports of President Lincoln's assassination. Her curiosity was piqued: how would they have heard that news and how long would it have taken; what would it have meant to them? She vividly remembered the moment fifteen years earlier when she had learned of President John F. Kennedy's assassination. She recalled how quickly that news had traveled and how dramatic it was: a shock wave across America.

So what began as a cocktail party question—"Where were you and how did you feel when you heard the news of President Kennedy's assassination?"— evolved into a five-year effort to document the memories of family, friends, and ultimately a broad spectrum of society. Intuitively Jodie knew that people would remember. Nearly everyone she asked recalled the most mundane details of their whereabouts, the disorienting sadness they experienced, and their feelings about how the world changed that day.

Working in the early 1980s, Jodie was ahead of the story-collecting curve. While Studs Terkel had legitimized oral history, story-collecting was not yet commonplace as either a tool for interpreting history or as entertainment. Jodie picked a topic with near universal relevance, and tapped into the deep desire we all have to place ourselves in history by sharing our personal narrative.

Fifty years after November 22, 1963, the iconography of that long weekend is cemented in the American psyche: Jackie's bloodstained suit; Walter Cronkite in his shirtsleeves, faltering when announcing the President's death; LBJ's swearing-in on Air Force One; the live television broadcast of Jack Ruby shooting Lee Harvey Oswald; the riderless horse in the funeral cortege; John Jr.'s salute. The memories in Jodie's collection—peppered with descriptive detail and ruminations on the implications of the President's violent death— offer an added dimension to this story. And they humanize the historical themes of the Kennedy era: civil rights, communism and the Cold War, the space program and the Peace Corps, the beginnings of the Vietnam War and the tumultuous "sixties" to come.

Expressions of shock and grief are juxtaposed with reports from parts of the country and the political spectrum decidedly not enamored with President Kennedy—responses of glee and satisfaction, cheering schoolchildren. Accounts from government officials and military personnel recount the actions necessary to secure an orderly transition of power. Civil rights activists and avowed liberals wonder: Who is LBJ? What's next for us? Kennedy's friends and peers speak of personal pain amidst the greater loss of an admired world leader.

In his 1978 memoir *In Search of History*, Theodore H. White writes, "The moments of history that crease the memory are rare, but come more frequently in our time than a hundred years ago because communications are instant. A triad of memories marks my generation: the strike at Pearl Harbor; the death of Franklin Roosevelt; the killing of John F. Kennedy. Each of us could write his own history of our time if we could but recall not where we were, which all remember, but what we thought when those accidents changed our world."

On November 22, 1963, "instant communications" meant broadcast reports of the shooting in Dallas interrupting soap operas on the three television networks. Then the world literally stood by, waiting to learn whether or not the President would live. The news then traveled quickly by telephone. Overloaded switchboards is a recurring theme—*The New York Times* received 31,800 calls that weekend from people seeking confirmation. The news was delivered by waiters and secretaries, by housewives calling husbands at work, and by stranger to stranger sharing transistor radios, or in one case, by a deaf woman reading the lips of broadcasters to a group of New Yorkers watching television through a store window. Because of television's continual coverage of the tragedy, Americans were eyewitnesses to history in an unprecedented way, especially the millions who watched the live broadcast of Oswald's murder.

Fifty years later, all that feels quaint, as we navigate a world of truly instant communications, in which tragedy and our reactions to it are immediately and relentlessly recorded. For my generation the "moment of history that crease(s) the memory" is September 11, 2001. In the days and weeks following that terrible day, those of us who experienced it coped by telling our stories, over and over, and making 9/11 the most extensively documented catastrophe in history.

Our information age is fast and furious, and saturated with personal narrative. In a world in which our every thought can be—and often is—widely shared within moments of conception, Jodie's letters are jarringly old-fashioned. On formal letterhead, with their apologies for tardy responses and typing errors, these letters portray a bygone era. But the narratives themselves, with their ruminations on lost innocence and ambivalence about the future, are eerily familiar and comforting as we endeavor to make sense of a turbulent world.

Jodie's collection is an assemblage of famous, infamous, and ordinary people who answered an earnest query from an unpublished, uncredentialed small-town nurse. From Phyllis Diller to Daniel Patrick Moynihan, from J. D.

Watson to Julia Child, the letters from prominent people are surprisingly intimate and sincere. Hank Aaron and Stan Musial took Jodie's calls, while Colonel Sanders called her to report he couldn't remember his whereabouts that day. There were a handful of obvious form letters—then-Vice President George H. Bush slipped in a campaign plug—but for the most part, people took her seriously. She rounded out those big names with hundreds of questionnaires to, and interviews with, teachers, students, doctors, laborers, soldiers, and housewives, people of various political persuasions, and from different parts of the country and the world.

After collecting stories from family and friends, in 1979 Jodie lucked upon an in-person interview with entertainer Danny Thomas while he was visiting St. Jude Children's Research Hospital, which he had founded, in Memphis. In his enthusiasm for the project, Thomas suggested she write to his celebrity friends, Hollywood stars like George Burns, Bob Hope, and Douglas Fairbanks, Jr. She did, and they wrote back. She then began writing to a wider array of politicians, academics, journalists, scientists, artists, and world leaders.

Jodie carefully followed current events, sending out dozens of new requests each week. With *Time* magazine as her guide, she wrote to people from a variety of fields, especially those with a connection to Kennedy's administration or to the issues which defined his presidency. The responses poured in—even people with no memory, or no wish to share one, politely replied and often congratulated her on her unique enterprise.

On her daily trips to the post office, her anticipation was shared by the postal workers. They were having nearly as much fun as she was, as letters arrived from around the world to the little post office in Union City, Tennessee. They marveled over the movie star signatures and a demented rant from Charles Manson, were aghast when Jodie became an unwitting subscriber to Yasser Arafat's PLO magazine, and generally cheered her on.

She carried her tape recorder into a national security conference at Ole Miss, featuring former Secretary of State Dean Rusk. She attended the 1978 Democratic mini-convention in Memphis, at which Edward Kennedy stole the show from President Jimmy Carter. She visited Buddhist monks, PT boaters, a Mennonite community, and attended rural church revival meetings.

My sisters and I occasionally accompanied her on excursions to track down stories, and once nervously waited in the car parked outside the Tennessee State Prison, while Jodie worked with the warden to record accounts from death row inmates. When she received the handwritten letter from Charles Manson, we took notice, but mostly, our Mom's collection of "Kennedy letters" was just another of her quirky schemes that populated our childhood—a pediatric surgical bandage innovation, the invention of a board game, batiking in the backyard, banjo lessons.

In 2011, Jodie and I revisited her project. With the fiftieth anniversary of the assassination approaching, we knew there would be grand, sweeping interpretations of the event's impact. There would be a resurgence of interest in conspiracy theories, and there would be new analyses of Kennedy's politics and legacy.

We sat down with her seven hundred stories, and I was drawn to two letters from Robert Penn Warren, the Pulitzer Prize–winning novelist. They are dated one month apart, and are nearly identical: a short paragraph conveying, by his own admission, a not especially interesting account of how he heard the news. "Why do you have two letters from Robert Penn Warren?" I asked. "I thought he could do better," she answered.

It was still quirky and idiosyncratic, but I had come to appreciate the appeal of my mother's work. I knew she had a resource that shed an entirely different light on the assassination, the Kennedys, and America.

Jodie had planned a book using first-person narratives to convey the drama of that day and its larger meaning. Instead, the letters she received and the stories she collected were so compelling as raw material, she decided to let them speak for themselves. This compilation is the best of those stories. It is also a historical document, a window onto a different era, a fun read, and not least, a tribute to my mother, whose desire to understand the seminal event that shaped her generation gives us a unique portrait of November 22, 1963.

JODIE USED THIS QUESTIONNAIRE AT THE START OF HER PROJECT.

We are publishing a book about the memories people have of an unexpected, dramatic, and tragic event in American history. The book will be compiled of personal stories submitted by people of all walks of life, people of all nationalities, and of all political party preferences-----telling us where they were, what they were doing, the feelings they had, the reaction of others around them, and how they heard the news of the assassination of the late President John F. Kennedy. The book will not be about his life or his politics. It will be about people and will be one of human interest as well as being historically significant. We have heard from all types of people -----educators, businessmen, lawyers, doctors, housewives, politicians, factory workers, authors, entertainers, etc. We are interested in your story and any small detail you remember will be important and significant.

Mrs Jodie Elliott Hansen
Box 1031
Union City, Tennessee 38261

Full Name_____ Age_____

Current Address_____ Address Nov. '63_____

Occupation or Profession now_____
Occupation or Profession Nov. '63_____
Use space below and please include small details, such as: if you saved any newspaper clippings or memorial publications; if you had ever seen or met President Kennedy; if you (at the time) were worried or apprehensive about the possibility of a world crisis or a conspiracy; if your community had any special church or memorial services, etc. Any small detail is important.

Use back of paper, if more space needed----and for any philosophical comments or historical insight you have, concerning the event.

"When luminaries such as James Michener, General Mark Clark, and Reverend The-odore Hesburgh responded to my original questionnaire, I realized I was asking a question people were eager to answer. I began to write personal letters, and as my list of responders grew, I did some rather blatant name-dropping in order to collect more." . . .

Senator Ted Kennedy has given me a comment or two pertaining to this tragic event. I also have letters from former Governor John Connally, former President George Bush, Senator Barry Goldwater, former Governor George Wallace, Senator Julian Bond, former Senator Margaret Chase Smith, U.S. Secretary of Agriculture Bob Bergland, and Lynn Greenwalt who is the director of the U.S. Fish and Wildlife Service.

Mayor Koch of New York City has responded and Henry Ford II sent me a copy of the statement he had given to the press on November 22, 1963. Former Secretary of State Dean Rusk who was en route to Japan with other Cabinet members; Judge Sarah Hughes, who administered the presidential oath to Lyndon Johnson; and others who were in Dallas including several newsmen have sent accounts of this dramatic day in their lives. The British Broadcasting Company (BBC) sent the transcript of a documentary program they did in 1976 and Lowell Thomas has sent the transcript of his broadcast concerning this historic event.

General Maxwell Taylor, Mrs. Lyndon Johnson, Leon Jaworski, Jack Valenti, and former President Gerald Ford have sent very courteous letters and have referred me to their books (written several years after this event) for their personal memories.

Princess Grace of Monaco has shared her memories of how she first heard the news. Mrs. Indira Gandhi sent me an interesting letter and Lord C. P. Snow has also responded.

People from other countries along with Americans who lived outside the United States in 1963 have responded. One woman who was living in Paris at the time heard the initial report on Voice of America and while waiting for additional news, heard the guns of the École Militaire firing the official salute to the dead chief of state. A man who was in the jungles of South America was told the news in a very matter-of-fact way by a white mercenary soldier who had recently returned from fighting in the Congo; a man in the Air Force helped load bombs and missiles—just in case…; and a vice-admiral in the Navy was on a submarine near Scotland.

Many college presidents and professors from all over the country have had very interesting philosophical comments and historical insights concerning this event. Peace Corps volunteers, PT veterans, and prisoners (one on death row at the time) have sent accounts. The Vatican sent a copy of Pope Paul VI's statement to the press.

A Memphis newsman heard the news in a most unusual way. He was in New York City and noticed a large crowd gathered in front of a television retail sales outlet store. The people were watching the TV sets through the store windows but could not hear what the news commentators were saying. A deaf lady in the crowd read the lips of the newsmen and told the people around her that the President had been shot.

A couple from Mississippi had ordered a new rocking chair (sometimes known as a "Kennedy rocker") and were unpacking it in front of their television set when the news was announced. The lady wrote on the bottom of the chair, "This is the day President John F. Kennedy was shot." Today, after almost seventeen years, the words are still there.

In addition to these examples, entertainers, sports figures, and others who are eminent in their fields have responded. I've received letters from George Burns, Steve Allen, Hal Holbrook, Ned Beatty, Oleg Cassini, Arthur Ashe, Art Linkletter, and Mr. and Mrs. Roy Rogers.

NOVEMBER 22, 1963

BARBARA MEANS ADAMS, *Oglala Sioux author*

November 22, 1980

Dear Mrs Hansen:

I feel very fortunate that you asked me to write something for you. Even after 17 years, I remember so well the death of the President.

This poem formed over the years and I've really had a reason to finish it.

This is what actually happened to us and others on Pine Ridge Indian Reservation, South Dakota. My home was Wounded Knee, So. Dak. I am from the Oglala Sioux Tribe.

Sincerely
Barbara (Means) Adams

(continued)

IN MEMORY OF J. F. KENNEDY

22ND, NOV. 1963

At the moment of his going, the streams
Flowed quietly; the Trading Post was deserted.
Ghostly snow flakes sprinkled the grass
Mercury sank in the mouth of the sunset
The afternoon of his death was a dark, cold day.

Branches wept as the Autumn frost perched
The drip of the dew broke off all dreams
Minds were stunned, tongues couldn't find words
As the owl in the pine trees cried thrice.

His widow stood with streaming eyes
Gazed upon the husband of her youth
With anguish none could paint or tell
She drew his every trait to her.

Grandfather paced with closed fists
His shadow fell upon the lighted ceiling
He peered out from heavy eye brows
He was still a man in green uniform
His head gray and all, was thrown back.

In reverence and awe, Grandmother lit
Candles before the President's picture
Their wax tears dripped for him all night
Straining to shine brighter in the morning.

Leaning against the stairs near the door
Nothing was with me but the sound of
The President's voice two days earlier
On the radio far from the State Capitol.

"It is Hope for a hemisphere of natives
Where every man has enough to eat
A chance to work and every child can learn
Every family can find decent shelter.
It is for a hemisphere where every man can
Be liberated from bonds of Social Injustice
Free to pursue his own talents and allowed
To participate in the fruits of progress."

Page two.

As if in a swoon, all things became confused
In every church along Wounded Knee valley
I saw a bright glow about the altars
And black palls and flowers in a row
And dozens of faces all in tears
As the last words of the President's
Undelivered, Dallas Speech were repeated,
"Peace on Earth, Good Will Toward Men."

The few scant moments left on T.V. were a dream
As the procession suddenly emerged from a mist
Bearing crosses and smoking incense
Mother and two children; His son saluting
Two marine guards stared into space
A lone horse shook the leaves off his back
And scattered them like alms among the poor.

The voices near me, having sobbed their fill
Were more subdued. Their chanting of prayers
Floated out more and more faintly
As the horse's inwards heaved in answer
To the swish and clink of his shod hoofs
The afternoon of his funeral was a dark, cold day.

November 1980
Barbara Means Adams

DORIS HEREFORD ADKINSON *(in 1963) seventh grader in Smyrna, Tennessee*

One of the memories I have of the day President Kennedy died is that the suicide rate in America dropped dramatically that day. I either read it someplace or heard it on television but it does make sense because people's thoughts were on something other than themselves and they had the distraction of this national tragedy.

—————

AIR FORCE ONE, *unit history from November 21–25, 1963, written by the office of the presidential pilot*

Fifty jet fighters, each representing one of the 50 states of the union, escorted Air Force One as it passed over Arlington Cemetery just as President John F. Kennedy was being lowered in to the grave and Taps was being played. The Presidential jet dipped its wings in a final salute to the Commander-in-Chief. Air Force One had flown him 196,867 statute miles. Mrs. Kennedy had requested this special salute from the Presidential jet. "He loved that airplane so much," she said. "It took him to so many places.

EDWARD ALBEE
THE OFFICE
14 HARRISON STREET
NEW YORK, N. Y. 10013

July 4, 1983

Dear Mrs. Hansen:

Your letter of March 8th <u>did</u> arrive , and I answer it
only now on my return from a long travel.

To reply to your question: I was in Odessa, U.S.S.R., on
a cultural exchange visit (John Stienbeck and I going there
together) and I --plus my U.S. Embassy escort, William Luers,
later U.S. Ambassador to Venezuela -- had just been to the opera
there for a dreadful production of a minor Romsky-Korsakov
opera. We walked back from the opera house to the hotel, commenting on the peculiar strident quality of so many Russian sop-
ranos. When we entered the hotel we were startled to hear the
Voice of America (unjammed) announcing the shooting and death
of Kennedy. The lobby, and the great stairs of the hotel, were
filled with disbelieving and weeping people --U.S. and other.
I recall being more homesick and lonely than ever before or
since in my life.

Regards,

    Edward Albee

Carl Albert
Federal Building
Third and Carl Albert Parkway
McAlester, Oklahoma 74501

May 3, 1983

Mrs. Jodie Elliott Hansen
Box 1031
Union City, Tennessee 38261

Dear Mrs. Hansen:

This is in response to your letter of April 27, 1983.

I was standing in the Oval Room of the White House talking to President Kennedy as he was about to leave on his ill-fated trip to Dallas. His helicopter had just landed. I was Majority Leader of the House of Representatives at this time. After the President and I had talked briefly about the Legislative matters in Congress the President stood, shook hands with me, looked out of the window towards his helicopter. This was the last time I ever saw him. I remember the occasion distinctly. He stood on his toes a couple of times with his back towards me and left.

About noon I was eating my lunch alone in the Congressional Hotel. One of the secretaries of the Committee on Agriculture who was eating in a small adjacent room jumped up and came over to me. She asked if I had heard what the radio in the other room had just said. When I told her I had not, she said a report had just come in that President Kennedy had been shot in Dallas. She told me there was no report as to whether he was living or dead. I was stunned. I jumped up from my table and went to my office immediately. When I got there the phone was ringing. Ted Sorenson was calling. He told me that the President was dead. It was an awful day.

In the evening I went to Andrews Field where the body of the late President was flown in. A little later I was with President Johnson over at the Executive Office Building. Three or four other Congressmen were with us. I remember that one was Congressman Homer Thornberry. I think Congressman Jack Brooks was another. No one said much. I remember President Johnson telling me later that he made up

his mind during that short walk that for the rest of his life he would "call them as he saw them."

When I went home that night my seven year old son, David, had tears in his eyes. President Kennedy was a great favorite of his. Only a short time before, while David and some of his cousins were visiting with me in the White House, the President had taken a PT boat tie clasp off of his tie and fastened it on David's.

These are all vivid recollections regarding events of that day.

Sincerely,

Earl Albert

CA/sk

STEVE ALLEN
15201 BURBANK BOULEVARD
SUITE B
VAN NUYS, CALIFORNIA 91411
(213) 988-3830

First
November
1979

Mrs. Jodie Elliott Hansen
Box 1031
Union City, TN 38261

Dear Mrs. Hansen,

Your letter of October 6th was most interesting and I'm sure
your book will be the same.

I was asleep in our home in Los Angeles the morning the news
of the President's assassination came. I can't recall at the
moment whether our housekeeper or my wife Jayne awakened me.
We all turned on the bedroom television set at once and then
-- like practically everyone else in the nation -- sat stunned
and horrified as details of the tragic event were communicated.
Oddly enough my mind went back to the moment -- was it in 1944?
-- that I heard the radio news flash about the death of President
Franklin Roosevelt. I was working at radio station KMTR in
Los Angeles at the time and recall being surprised at the news.
Tears welled up in my eyes even though I was on on-the-air duty at
the time.

The same emotion, as I say, gripped me when I learned of the
death of President Kennedy although in this instance I did not
weep since the information came as such a shock as to induce
an emotional state partially characterized by numbness broken
by flickering attempts at disbelief.

There were also moments of what I suppose must have been vengeful
response, and anger at the perpetrator or perpetrators, whoever
they might be.

The only other detail that might be relevant to your research came a few days later when the television networks gave extended coverage to the president's funeral and burial. Our son Bill, who was about three at the time, did not understand about video-tape repeats and assumed -- reasonably enough within the context of the knowledge he had -- that if he saw a news event on tele-vision it was actually happening. When, for what must have been the third or fourth time, he saw the video-tape footage of the coffin being lowered into the ground he ran to me saying, "Daddy, they're burrying the president again."

My last recollection of an emotional response to the assassination of President Kennedy came either the day of the dreadful event or shortly thereafter when I was astonished to hear that in a reactionary school a mem-ber of a particular religious faith announced the news to her students, who applauded! That one instance -- God help us -- reveals a depressing and perplexing truth about   political passions.

I look forward to reading your study when it is published.

Cordially,

Steve Allen

SA:ds

NEILL ARMSTRONG, *professional football player and coach*

CHICAGO BEARS

March 19, 1980

Mrs. Jodie Elliott Hansen
Box 1031
Union City, Tennessee 38261

Dear Mrs. Hansen:

Your letter regarding your book was received just last week. Thus, the delay in responding.

To the best of my recollection, this was what took place in my life on that sad, eventful day in history, 1962.

At the time, I was a coach for the Houston Oilers of the American Football League. At the conclusion of practice, someone broke the news that our President, John F. Kennedy, had been shot in Dallas, Texas. What I heard was hard to accept and immediately began to pray for his life to be spared. A friend of mine, another coach, and I, showered, dressed and started our drive through congested traffic, homeward. We, with thousands of others in the Houston area, continued to listen via radio to the reports of his progress. Still in a state of disbelief, I thought back to another point in time, to the assassination of another President, Abraham Lincoln. That another such event had taken place in my lifetime was unbelievable.

The office of the President of the United States is, was and will always be respected by me as one of greatness in every way. John F. Kennedy was a man that filled this office with dignity and to see his life taken in such a manner, was tragic, and this country will forever be saddened by his death.

I pray that the office of the President of the United States will never again experience such an event.

These are the things that I remember on that day in November, 1962.

My sincere best wishes to you.

Sincerely yours,

Neill Armstrong
Head Coach

RICHARD ARRINGTON, JR., *civil rights leader,*
Mayor of Birmingham, Alabama

RICHARD ARRINGTON, JR.
MAYOR

City of Birmingham, Alabama

OFFICE OF THE MAYOR

February 1, 1984

Mrs. Jodie Elliott Hansen
Box 1031
Union City, TN 38261

Dear Mrs. Hansen:

Thank you for allowing me the opportunity to share with you some details of what I was doing and my initial reaction to the death of President John F. Kennedy.

I was in attendance at a statewide science program at the University of Oklahoma in Norman. As I walked into the room where the seminar was being held, I noticed that a number of students were viewing a television set with great attention. In an effort to determine what had so completely captured their attention, I went forward only to discover the awful truth. The young president, who many of us in this nation and the world viewed with so much admiration, had been slain.

I was deeply saddened as I was optimistic that Mr. Kennedy's administration would get the nation moving in the right direction. Indeed, he had inspired us all. He had given us hope. He had shared a vision with all America that was at once idealistic but at the same time pragmatic. Certainly as a black person, I had dreams that with Kennedy's election we could now look to the White House to right many of the wrongs that I felt were unjustly visited upon blacks all over this land. But now this dream was all over; it had degenerated into a nightmare!

I was stunned and angered. My first reaction was to apportion blame, but I quickly discovered that I knew of no one to fault for this tragedy. I experienced a feeling of emptiness; of hurt that was beyond measure. Mercifully, as time wore on, this feeling of quiet anger and sadness began to subside but not disappear. To this very day, "That day in Dallas" troubles me whenever I think of what might have been had Mr. Kennedy lived to implement his policies which I firmly supported.

Sincerely,

Richard Arrington, Jr.
Mayor

RA/lwf

May 28, 1981

Mrs. Jodie Elliott Hansen
Box 1031
Union City, TN 38261

Dear Mrs. Hansen,

I think your idea of writing a book compiling the personal accounts from all
over the world of people´s responses to President Kennedy´s assassination is
good one. This will be especially interesting as the years go by.

I remember it as if it were yesterday. It was so shocking to have it happen
right here in Dallas. We were all very excited about the President coming t
Dallas and crowds lined the streets all the way from the airport. I was at
work that day -- our Company was two months old. We opened on September 13,
1963, and we were located in the mall of Exchange Bank Park, two doors from
the stock market. They, of course, received the news first, and came down a
told us. The entire Mall took on a shocked, hushed attitude as people learn
the news, and we were all glued to the television set to hear what happened.
That such a bazaar thing could happen to such a beloved man was impossible,
and the most shocking thing of all was that it happened here in our city.
The man, of course, who shot the President was not a Dallasite, for which we
were all grateful. I can only tell you that for days afterwards everyone wa
in a state of depression at losing our President, but worst of all, having i
happen here. I guess that´s about all I can tell you. Even today as I thin
back on it, I feel so very sad because President Kennedy was such a wonderfu
man, and it was such a tragic, useless act.

I hope that there is some part of this that you can use. Much good luck to
you on your book. I also have a book coming out in September called, The Ma
Kay Story. Harper and Row is publishing it.

Cordially,

Mary Kay

Mary Kay
Chairman of the Board

MKA:jpj

Mary Kay COSMETICS
®
Mary Kay Ash
Chairman of the Board
8787 Stemmons Freeway
Dallas 75247

5 October 1981

Dear Mrs. Hansen,

In my case, you will find the story of my interaction with the Kennedy assassination on pages 324 and 325 of the second volume of my autobiography: IN JOY STILL FELT. You are welcome to reprint it without charge (but with the usual acknowlegements of copyright.)

Isaac Asimov

EDWARD ASNER

February 3, 1982

Mrs. Jodie Elliott Hansen
Box 1031
Union City, Tennessee 38261

Dear Mrs. Hansen:

Thank you for your letter about your book on the Kennedy assassination.

At the time I heard, I was filming the TV pilot for "Slattery's People," which co-starred Richard Crenna. We were in Sacramento, and the news came to us off the ticker tape on the floor of the Assembly. We did not continue shooting that day and, of course, we were all aghast at the news.

I hope this is what you need--best of luck with your project.

Sincerely,

Ed Asner

Edward Asner

kk

ROMY AYCOCK *(in 1963) resident of Union City, Tennessee*

Chicago was like a ghost town, not the usual hustle and bustle. Stores were closed. Theaters were closed. The atmosphere at the old LaSalle Hotel was gloomy. Everywhere you looked, the people were solemn and sad.

———

TERRY BAGGETT *(in 1963) in training for the Peace Corps*

I remember being a little surprised that many of the stores and businesses there (in Boston) were open per usual, although Kennedy's picture was in many store and shop windows. I also remember hearing a cannon in the Boston Common being fired many times, I think every hour....We rented a car on Sunday and were at Walden Pond when a complete stranger ran up to us with the news about Jack Ruby killing Lee Harvey Oswald.

TAWFIK BAILONY *(in 1963) seventh grader living in Syria*

10/15/78

It was ~~our~~ 15 years ago when it happened, I still remember that day, I was living in Syria, in the seven grade, a lot of hope was put on John F. Kennedy to resolve the Middle East problem, it seemed to me and the people of that area that J.F.K is the first strong U.S. presendent who is ~~apf~~ able to say or try to say to Isreal what is wrong and what is wright. It was noon, sitting in a public bus and coming back from school when I heard the news, and my first thing I said", they killed him. the Jews killed him because they don't want any peace in that area

Now Iam M.D., things changed and time passed and may need more time to know the truth.

Dr Tawfik Bailony
8414 Rockcreek
Cordova TN
38018

28

R O S S R. B A R N E T T, *Governor of Mississippi*

B A R N E T T, M O N T G O M E R Y, M c C L I N T O C K & C U N N I N G H A M
ATTORNEYS AT LAW
SUITE 315-321 BARNETT BUILDING
JACKSON, MISSISSIPPI 39205

ROSS R. BARNETT
GEORGE T. McCLINTOCK
E. HUGH CUNNINGHAM, JR.
ROSS R. BARNETT, JR.
G. WILLIAM PALMER
ROBERT C. GRENFELL
JOHN H. BARNETT, III

December 31, 1979

M. B. MONTGOMERY
(1891-1975)

P. O. BOX 1288
AREA CODE 601
TELEPHONE 948-6640

Mrs. Jodie Elliott Hansen
Box 1031
Union City, TN   38261

Dear Mrs. Hansen:

Thanks for your letter of recent date.

President Kennedy was a good friend of mine, and I
admired him greatly. He was the best of all of the
Kennedy family. He was always courteous and kind to me.

I was making a talk at a Rotary Club in Aberdeen,
Mississippi, when the news came there. I announced it
to the members of the club and then I went back to
Jackson and prepared to go to Washington to the funeral.
Several of us went in an Army plane.

President Kennedy was a man of courage and great
energy, a man of integrity, a man who was trustworthy,
and it was indeed a great tragedy that he lost his life.

Sincerely yours,

ROSS R. BARNETT

RRB/da

Birch Bayh, *U.S. Senator from Indiana*

Bayh, Tabbert & Capehart
Attorneys at Law

BIRCH E. BAYH
DON A. TABBERT
JAMES B. CAPEHART
THOMAS A. CONNAUGHTON
RICHARD J. DARKO
DANIEL F. EVANS, JR.
STEPHEN J. HARMS
M. KENT NEWTON
JAMES V. ELLIOTT
JOEL YONOVER
ROBERT B. KEENE
MICHAEL W. WELLS
RICHARD I. FORD
ROBERT R. CLARK
THOMAS M. HINSHAW
JAMES T. SMITH
BERNARD L. PYLITT
KEVIN O. FALEY
JANET C. KNAPP
BRIAN W. FITZGERALD

INDIANAPOLIS OFFICE
ONE INDIANA SQUARE
SUITE 2410
INDIANAPOLIS, IN 46204
(317) 639-5444

WASHINGTON OFFICE
1575 EYE STREET, N.W.
SUITE 1025
WASHINGTON, DC 20005
(202) 289-8660

July 1, 1982

Mrs. Jodie Elliott Hansen
Box 1031
Union City, Tennessee 38261

Dear Mrs. Hansen:

In response to your letter of April 8, 1982, I am sharing my memories of the day that President John Kennedy was assassinated. I spent the morning with Postmaster General John A. Gronouski and then went to the Pentagon to meet with Secretary of Defense Robert McNamara, telling them I had to talk to John Kennedy and Robert Kennedy about the contracts for postal vehicles with Studebaker in South Bend, Indiana. Studebaker was going out of business and negotiations were underway for International Harvester to take over their operations. I called Bob Kennedy from the airport and told him I was going to Chicago to talk to the president of International Harvester to see if they would assume the running of the Studebaker plant and honor the Studebaker contract, but before I did that I wanted to make sure the administration would still support that. Bob said the President wanted that done.

The plane to Chicago bounced around in a driving rainstorm and we had to take two passes at the runway before we could land. Right before we landed, the Captain told the passengers that President Kennedy had been assassinated. The response was that of disbelief; the passengers were stunned. A panorama of experiences with President Kennedy crossed my mind and a concern for the future of his family and our country came into play. In reflecting, it seemed that the heavens had opened up with tears for our great loss.

Mrs. Jodie Elliott Hansen
July 1, 1982
Page two

     I hope that these comments will be of some value to you
as you compile personal accounts from people all over the world
for your book. I appreciate your including my thoughts with
others and wish you much success with your publication.

                    Sincerely,

                    Birch Bayh

BB:ah

FIELD NEWSPAPER SYNDICATE

2926 Garfield Street

Betty Beale

Washington, D.C.   20008

June 22, 1982

Mrs. Jodie Elliott Hansen
Box 1031
Union City, Tenn. 38261

Dear Mrs. Hansen:

Forgive this long delay in replying to your letter of May 6.

I was put into a most unusual position by the death of President Kennedy. I had gone to New York at the request of my syndicate—then the Hall Syndicate—to tape a pilot commentary on the Kennedys. The syndicate had decided that some of its columnists might be used for very brief spots on TV wherever they might be worked in—probably on news shows.

I had written something about the Kennedys' style in the White House in a couple of minutes, though I do not recall now the exact time.

I had run through it a couple of times but had paused or done something wrong so it had to be done again when the news came in that John Kennedy had been shot and might be dead. Needless to say, the divine ways the Kennedys entertained had to be scotched immediately.

As the recording studio and technicians had been hired for a sample TV spot and I had gone up to New York for that purpose only, I was asked if I could come up at once with a piece on White House social life under the Johnsons. I said I had been to several of their parties (I had known them since he was majority leader of the Senate) and thought I could.

I went into another room to concentrate and gather my thoughts. There wasn't time for me to write something out. There wasn't time to mourn the assassination of a young president. I do not remember if the technicians had another commitment or what. I just remember I had to produce something in a hurry.

So while the rest of the world was reeling from the tragedy I was trying my darnedest to project myself into the next year or longer in the White House with the Johnsons, visualizing the pep LBJ, that human dynamo, would stimulate at even state functions, the friendly, easygoing warmth and hospitality Lady Bird would instill in every gathering. Yes, while everyone else was engulfed in grief I had to talk about the lively dancing parties that would prevail because once the White House was restored to normal I knew President Johnson's love for dancing would mean that dance

401 NORTH WABASH AVE.   CHICAGO, ILL. 60611   TELEPHONE (312) 321-2795

music would be added to evening functions. The Kennedys generally limited dancing to their private parties, which were big, glamorous affairs. The Johnsons had no private dancing parties.

That whole studio experience was unreal and, understandably, led to nothing. I could not do under those circumstances and off the cuff the kind of smooth performance required for television. And it may be that the recipients of the pilot, if any, took a dim view of a commentary about the gaiety of the LBJ administration while they were still grief-stunned about the assassination.

Such is the life of a reporter. We have to adopt the king-is-dead-long-live-the-king attitude. When I returned to Washington that same Friday, November 22, 1963, I found that my newspaper, the Washington Star, had been calling frantically because my Sunday column, submitted Wednesday was all about the Kennedys. They wanted a new column sent down that very evening on the social White House under the Johnsons. So again I had no time to think about the tragedy. It was not till I went to the White House when Kennedy's casket lay in state in the East Room that I experienced the impact of the assassination.

I hope all this gives you what you wanted to know.

Sincerely yours,

Betty Beale

BETTY BEALE

NED BEATTY, *actor*

May 11, 1979

Mrs. Jodie Elliott Hansen
Box 1031 803 E. Exchange Street
Union City, Tennessee 38261

Dear Jodie,

Thank you for your letter. I'm pleased to hear from Fritz again. Tell him for me please that I hope to see him soon.

Your project about John F. Kennedy and where and what people were doing and the feelings they had on the day that he was assinated is an interesting sounding one. I, of course, like the others that you have contacted remember pretty clearly what I was doing that day.

I was working at the Arena Stage in Washington, D.C., re-hearsing a play that day called "Say Nothing"...a rather off-beat piece by an English novelist playwrite whose name I don't recall. I remember having a feeling of disbelief in the news that I had heard; wondering if it just wasn't perhaps a hysterical rumor. There was such polarization during that period in Washington between people who were pro-civil rights and those who weren't and I must say that being from a border state like Kentucky, I was sensi-tive about those kind of feelings and the kind of feelings of the people I lived around had towards anyone from the south. Since President Kennedy was in Dallas there obvi-ously was some ill feeling towards him in that part of the country.

My first thought was, "Perhaps this is a rumor that someone has started to besmear the name of the south and southernors." I remember not wanting to take the news seriously and wanted to continue rehearsing the play. It was a very interesting play and I had quite an involved, difficult role in it.

Later, when the news came through again...the fact that the fear was that not only had he been shot at, but that he had been hit and he was indeed not going to survive, my feeling basically was one of dismay at living in a society where someone could be shot because of his title. I wasn't a great Kennedy fan I suppose, so I wasn't having any kind of strong personal feelings or any sense of personal loss or loss of someone that I held in great high regard. I don't think I really liked too much the sort of Camelot on the front page news coverage of he and his family that we were getting every day during that period.

I was mainly shocked and dismayed that anyone would take someone's life basically because of the position that they are in. I had a strange feeling about that. I'm not sure I accept the conclusions of the Warren Commission on who was responsible basically because of personal things that have happened to me in my life in my travels in that area, in Dallas and so forth.

I originally accepted the Warren Commission report and figured that Oswald was just an oddball who had taken a shot at a power figure; who was an authoritarian paranoid or whatever but then again, now, I'm not so sure. I'm not sure what was shot down that day. The bottom line is that I think I have a sense that what was shot down was the possibilities for change that John F. Kennedy was presenting. I think over these last years we have been getting back to the point where we can look to change again.

I hope this is useful to you in your research.

Love to you and all of yours.

Regards,

Ned Beatty

NB:kg

RALPH BELLAMY, *actor*

RALPH BELLAMY
8173 MULHOLLAND TERRACE
LOS ANGELES, CALIF. 90046

March 22,1980

Dear Mrs. Hansen:

In reply to your letter
of March 12 I am submitting the enclosed.
I hope you can find it useful. It's probably
similar to other reactions in other areas
of preoccupation at the time word came.

I also have a recollection
of news of the death of F.D.R.--I was in a
bar in New York with my lawyer. It was the
end of the day and commuters on their way
to Grand Central Station had stopped for
a quick one. They were standing four deep
and a radio was going softly on top of the
cash register. Suddenly, over the din of
hurried conversation came the words. "President Roosevelt is dead!"

There was silence, except
for the ring of the cash register--the continuing news-cast and the shuffling of feet.

In no time at all the bar
was empty.

Good luck with the book.
I've recently had one published myself.

Sincerely

RALPH BELLAMY
8173 MULHOLLAND TERRACE
LOS ANGELES, CALIF. 90046

The news flash of the assassination of
President Kennedy was relayed to us on
a sound stage at M.G.M. during the filming of the Tv series "11th Hour".

A radio was turned on and everyone in the
cast froze in their tracks. We stood like
statues. Some of the statues shed tears.

This was a man who inspired people--who
was admired by the entire free world. He
was the fulfillment of our hope for peace
and a new and strong and re-born America.

And now he was gone. Tragically--almost
theatrically. I still believe, the victim
of a plot.

After twenty minutes to a half hour the
producer of our series said to me "What
do you think we should do?" I thought a
minute, gathering my own composure, and
said "Well,I suppose the old show business
dictum,'The show must go on', applies here.
And maybe it would be good for us to put
our minds to something else."

We went back to work.

But we couldn't remember our lines. The
statues had come to life, but the minds
and emotions were still out of control.

So we went home.

MELVIN BELLI, *attorney and author, represented Jack Ruby*

SAN FRANCISCO, CALIFORNIA 94111
415 · YUKON 1-1849
The Belli Building   722 MONTGOMERY STREET

MELVIN M. BELLI
VASILIOS B. CHOULOS
JOHN E. KALIN
MORRIS BEATUS
FEDERICO CASTELAN SAYRE
THOMAS J. LoSAVIO
ROBERT A. MITCHELL
MICHAEL HARDY
DEBORAH B. HONIG
JETTIE PIERCE SELVIG
JUSTIN DWINNELL, III

CHIEF INVESTIGATOR
EUGENE J. MARSHALL

Law Offices
Belli & Choulos
Cable "Belos"

San Francisco – March 31, 1981

LOS ANGELES, CALIFORNIA 90048
213 · 653 · 4777
6300 WILSHIRE BOULEVARD SUITE 9000

MELVIN M. BELLI
VASILIOS B. CHOULOS
FEDERICO CASTELAN SAYRE
STEVEN D. ARCHER

Belli, Weil & Jacobs
202 · 857 · 0777
ONE CENTRAL PLAZA, S.W.10
11300 ROCKVILLE PIKE
ROCKVILLE, MARYLAND 20852
MELVIN M. BELLI
HENRY E. WEIL *
HARVEY A. JACOBS *
ALVIN M. EHRLICH *
*MEMBER CAL. BAR ONLY
*NOT MEMBER CAL. BAR

OF COUNSEL
DANNY JONES
NORWALK, CALIFORNIA

Mrs. Jodie Elliott Hansen
Box 1031
Union City, Tennessee 38261

Dear Mrs. Hansen:

I was trying a homicide case in Los Angeles when news came to the judge that President Kennedy was assassinated. He stood up and said "My God". The jurors all stood up, some cried, some became hysterical.

The judge said "We'll recess for the afternoon" and with that the district attorney and I went up to the head district attorney's office and looked at the TV news coming in from Dallas.

There were rumors and reports that it was a black man who did the killing, and I remember saying aloud "Oh God, I hope not." I was still trying the homicide case when Earl Ruby, Jack's brother, came out to watch me on trial in court, and after watching for a day, came up and asked me if I would represent his brother.

Best wishes,

MELVIN M. BELLI

MMB/kw

ROSEMARY BIGHEM *(in 1963) seventh grade teacher*

I was teaching history at an all-black school…I've had a lot of time to think about that day and the students' reaction. They had been caught up in that Kennedy aura and here was a man they could relate to, in a peculiar sort of way. He had said that black was not ugly and this man was going to bring about their salvation. He was a good man, he was white, and he was doing things that were favorable and made them feel that some of the elusive parts of America were going to be handed to them. Their grief, at that time, was genuine.

CHRISTA BOCK *(in 1963) living in West Berlin, Germany*

I was at home and was listening to music on the American Forces Network when the announcer interrupted the program with the news that the President of the United States of America, John F. Kennedy, had just been shot while visiting in Dallas, Texas….That night there were hundreds of thousands of Berliners who mourned his death by joining in the torchlight march which ended at the Schöneberg Rathaus (city hall) where a memorial service was held for our American friend. I remember that thousands of Berliners had candles in their window that night as a sign of mourning for the dead chief-of-state. I am not aware of any specific reason, political or otherwise, why the people of my country loved John F. Kennedy so much, but they liked him very much even before his visit there during the summer of 1963. When he gave his famous speech, his words, "Ich bin ein Berliner" just increased our endearment and affection for him.

Erma Bombeck, *humorist, syndicated columnist*

Erma Bombeck

August 31, 1981

Mrs. Jodie Elliott Hansen
Box 1031
Union City, Tennessee 38261

Dear Mrs. Hansen:

My memories of the assassination of
John Kennedy --

To begin with, it was not the best of all
days for a suburban housewife in Centerville, Ohio.

In one weekend, I had planned to host an
anniversary party for my parents and to chair a
church bazaar. To add to the drama, my husband
was having surgery to have two discs removed.

I figured if I lived through the weekend,
I could handle anything.

It began raining on that day and it never
stopped. When I returned from the school where
the bazaar was being set up, my mother told me
the President had been shot.

At the hospital, my husband was in the
recovery room when he heard the nurses talking.
That's all he talked about between his moments
of consciousness and sleep. He thought it was
all a bad dream.

My parents danced the Anniversary Waltz;
my husband recovered; the church bazaar netted
enough money to buy playground equipment; but
all of us knew we would never be the same after
that day. It's a prophecy I never wanted to
come true.

Erma Bombeck

Erma Bombeck

JULIAN BOND, *founder, Student Nonviolent Coordinating Committee,*
Georgia State Senator

JULIAN BOND
District 39
361 Westview Drive, S.W.
Atlanta, Georgia 30310

COMMITTEES:
Consumer Affairs
Governmental Operations
Human Resources, Vice Chairman
SUBCOMMITTEES:
Merit System
Aging

The State Senate

Atlanta, Georgia 30334

June 29, 1979

Mrs. Jodie Elliot Hansen
Box 1031
Union City, Tennessee 38261

Dear Mrs. Hansen:

I have discarded your questionaire but I hope what follows
will suffice.

I was eating lunch at Paschal's Restuarant on Atlanta's
Hunter Street (now M.L.K. Jr. Drive) with a journalist friend,
Mrs. Margaret Long, when a passerby remarked that the Presi-
dent had been shot.

This information was volunterred so calmly that we independently
assumed he'd been shot in the hand or foot; a frightening but
only temporary discomfort caused by some obviously deranged
person.

It was not until ½ hour (or more) later when I returned to
the offices of the Student Nonviolent Coordinating Committee
two blocks away that I learned the President had been assasi-
nated.

We, assorted SNCC workers, spent the rest of the 22nd calling
friends in Texas, trying to determine who Lyndon Johnson was,
and what he might mean to us and our work.

It was a sober, somber day. We were too afraid to cry.

I can remember a Black woman in rural Mississippi: remarking
that day "If they can do that to him, what won't they do to
us?"

Sincerely,

Julian Bond

JB/gg

WINFRIED BONSE, *member of staff to German Chancellor Helmut Schmidt*

PRESSE- UND INFORMATIONSAMT
DER BUNDESREGIERUNG
- IV A 3 -
46 626 h

53 BONN 1, den August 29,197
Postfach
Welckerstraße 11
Fernruf: 208–592
oder über Vermittlung 20 81
Fernschreiber: 0 886 741/743

Mrs. Jodie Elliott Hansen
803 E. Exchange Street
Union City, Tennessee 38261

U. S. A.

Dear Mrs. Elliott Hansen,

The Chancellory has asked me to thank you very much
for your letter of August 7, 1979. I regret to tell
you that the Chancellor because of his tight schedule
is unable to comply with your request. I do hope that
you understand this reply.

I know that the shock of the assassination of the late
President Kennedy only a few months after his successful
and impressive visit to the Federal Republic of Germany
is still alive in the memory of all Germans. I remember
well that after I heard the dreadful news in television
the whole country held its breath mourning for your
President. I watched people crying in the streets and
remember spontaneous gatherings of people especially
in Berlin in front of the Town Hall where President
Kennedy gave his famous speed only a short time before.

Sincerely,

(Winfried Bonse)

MRS. CECILE BOREAN *(in 1963) young woman shopping for her trousseau in Canada*

After making some selections, it seemed difficult to find a clerk, and the customers standing about appeared to be in a state of reverie. Finally a clerk was found. But this clerk, a woman of about fifty, was crying. The tears coursed down her cheeks and she didn't even make an effort to dry her eyes. "President Kennedy was shot," she sobbed....How could this happen? One person is rejoicing in anticipation of a very happy event while another one lies dead from an assassin's bullet. The world is shocked and stunned at the dreadful death of perhaps the most important leader in the whole world while one little insignificant human being lost in a huge department store tries to concentrate on a trousseau. How contradictory. How to reconcile the two events? How to pursue a happy quest when tragedy is so far-reaching and deeply felt? One event had no relationship to the other—and yet—the significance of the tragedy pales the anticipation of the celebration. What matters? Can one continue to assemble accessories with garments when a nation is bleeding? How insignificant one human being can become instantly in comparison to another and yet feel compassion for the greater. The events of the rest of that day seemed to have vanished. So many years later when I think of our wedding day, the event of November 23rd encroaches upon my memory—and seems more significant than our wedding.

GABOR BORITT, *historian, Lincoln scholar*

Full Name _Gabor S. Boritt_   Age _39_
Current Address _979 Audubon Dr Memphis TN_ Address Nov. '63 _Boston, Mass_
Occupation or Profession now _historian and teacher_
Occupation or Profession Nov. '63 _graduate student_
Use space below and please include small details, such as: if you saved any
newspaper clippings or memorial publications; if you had ever seen or met
President Kennedy; if you (at the time) were worried or apprehensive about
the possibility of a world crisis or a conspiracy; if your community had any
special church or memorial services, etc. **Any small detail is important.**

My memories of November 22, 1963, are clear in my mind —
perhaps excessively clear for I seem to relate them to my students
year after year.

I had taught some classes and worked at the library at Boston
University in the morning. In the afternoon I started for
home. I noticed nothing unusual on the street while waiting
for the streetcar. Presumably I was still absorbed in my
morning's reading on Lincoln. In the streetcar itself I
developed the strange feeling that something was wrong.
I put this down to my being very tired. In retrospect, however,
it appears that the 'total' silence of the streetcar and the
strained look on the passengers faces caused the feeling of strangeness.
This was Jack Kennedy's home town. I was on a streetcar to Brook-
line — his birthplace.

When I got home my mother opened the door. Her eyes were
swollen and she was crying when she said, in

her native Hungarian, "they killed the President."
Standing in the doorway I replied, with conviction:
"it could not be." But I have known death
in my life and even as I spoke I knew the truth.

CITY HALL
LOS ANGELES, CALIFORNIA 90012
(213) 485-3311

OFFICE OF THE MAYOR

TOM BRADLEY
MAYOR

August 3, 1981

Mrs. Jodie Elliott Hansen
Box 1031
Union City, Tennessee 38261

Dear Mrs. Hansen:

In response to your letter requesting information about what I
was doing at the time I first heard the news of the assassination
of President John F. Kennedy, I am sending the following account.

I was attending a City Council meeting; and one of the members of
the Council, Mrs. Rosalyn Wyman, came back from her office and
announced over the loudspeaker in the Council Chambers that
President Kennedy had been shot in Dallas. We all sat in stunned
silence for several seconds and then a motion was introduced to
adjourn the Council meeting.

I quickly returned to my office to get direct radio reports and
confirm the gravity of the situation. There was an eerie silence
which pervaded the entire City Hall and hardly any discussion
occurred between people. I felt a sense of emptiness and sorrow
which had been unmatched in my lifetime. I later went to my car
and simply drove around the streets of Los Angeles for more than
an hour. During that drive, I observed the look of disbelief on
the faces of everyone and witnessed an unreal quietness throughout
the City. Never have I felt such a sense of loss. The haunting
feeling will remain etched in my mind forever.

Very truly yours,

TOM BRADLEY
M A Y O R

TB/lt

**Republican
National
Committee**

August 6, 1979

Bill Brock
Chairman

Mrs. Jodie Elliott Hansen
Box 1031
803 East Exchange Street
Union City, Tennessee 38261

Dear Mrs. Hansen:

I was fascinated by your project to draw together some personal stories of those people who recall the news of the assassination of John Kennedy.

It's incredible how a very few days evoke such intense feelings and vivid memories. Two such days come very much to mind – one when I had just turned 11 years old and heard the news on a Sunday morning of the Japanese attack on Pearl Harbor. The other, of course, was that day when I heard the news of the assassination of President Kennedy.

On that particular day, I was scheduled to address a major political conference in Birmingham, Alabama. My mind was very much on the soon to be delivered speech as I left the airplane to be met by representatives of the sponsoring organization. They were obviously very much distraught and they told me that President Kennedy had just been shot in Dallas, Texas. I felt as though someone had hit me in the pit of the stomach. We tried to get more information at the airport, but no one could say with any certainty that he might live. On the contrary, the prognosis was uniformly reported as being virtually hopeless.

I had been in Congress less than a year and had no idea of what might be required of me or the Congress. I did know that the country would undergo an intense trauma in the ensuing hours and days.

Within about 45 minutes I was on a return flight to Washington with the obvious understanding and support of my host in having to cancel my appearance. The next hours were intensely personal and emotional. I don't know how to describe them except to say I wept and I prayed a great deal.

In all candor, it is impossible to sort out the pattern of thoughts which ran through my mind with such turbulence. I felt as though the country had been raped, that something very precious had been torn from our national fabric, and that it would take a great deal of goodness and decency to repair the wound. Most of all, they weren't really thoughts but feelings which only gradually were replaced with concerns about our political and social structure, and our national security.

I find it very difficult to elaborate further. Perhaps this will be helpful. Thank you for your interest in this project.

Very truly yours,

Bill Brock

BILL BROCK

BB:cb

Dwight D. Eisenhower Republican Center: 310 First Street Southeast, Washington, D.C. 20003. (202) 484-6500.

46

"The Lush"

1/30/82

Mrs. Jodie Elliott Hansen
Union City,
Tennessee

My dear Mrs. Hansen:

At the time of President Kennedy"s assassination
I was in the process of cleaning up around the
pool area of an apartment building which I was
managing at the time. This was long before I
met with the tremendous success I now enjoy in
show business.

When the news of the assassination came over the
radio in the court yard I was in shock as was
each tenant in the building as the news reached
them. While I was not the greatest booster of
President Kennedy and, did not vote for him, I
had to hold back the tears which was something
many of my tenants were unable to do.

President Kennedy was my President and I was
fast learning that he was doing all within his
power for the betterment of our country. I
think I would have cast my vote for him had he
not been taken from us.

Sincerely,

Foster Brooks

HELEN GURLEY BROWN, *editor of* Cosmopolitan *magazine*

Helen Gurley Brown, Editor · 224 West 57th Street, New York, New York, 10019, (212) 262-7916

January 22, 1980

Dear Mrs. Hansen,

On the day President Kennedy was assassinated, I
hadn't yet started working for Cosmopolitan and
was writing a book - SEX AND THE OFFICE. A friend
phoned to tell me the news and of course I didn't
get back to the book for a week. I was not an
avid John Kennedy supporter...somehow had not been
caught up in the magic with the rest of my friends
...had voted for Richard Nixon. I only felt the
tragedy that anyone would feel for a young life -
as well as that of possibly the most powerful man
in the world at that moment - being snuffed out so
senselessly and hideously.

All my best wishes,

Mrs. Jodie Elliott Hansen
Box 1031
Union City, Tennessee 38261

HGB:jed

COSMOPOLITAN IS A PUBLICATION OF HEARST MAGAZINES, A DIVISION OF THE HEARST CORPORATION

KING FEATURES SYNDICATE, INC.
235 East 45th Street
New York
New York 10017

March 12, 1982

Mrs. Jodie Elliott Hansen
Box 1031
Union City
Tennessee 38261

Dear Mrs. Hansen:

It must have been a Friday because on Fridays the
cartoonists who live in Connecticut used to bowl at the
Westport Bowlingalley on the Boston Port Road. There were
over a dozen of us, including Mort Walker (BEETLE BAILEY),
Bud Jones (MR. ABERNATHY), and Jack Tippett (AMY).

We had only bowled a few lines. My memory is that sometime after one o'clock someone came by to tell us that the
President had been shot. That ended the bowling--everyone
went home.

Jack Tippett, who lived in Westport, had the same
name as Officer Tippett who was killed in Dallas. He received
several calls from investigative agencies as well as a
certain amount of nasty phone calls. It's hard to explain this.
There is a certain sickness that seems to surface in the
wake of disasters.

I had not voted for Jack Kennedy but I remember crying
that day.

Sincerely,

Dik Browne

David W. Brubeck
221 *Millstone Road*
Wilton, Connecticut 06897
(203) 762-7710

May 25, 1982

Ms. Jodie Elliott Hansen
Box 1031
Union City, Tenn 38261

Dear Ms. Hansen:

Here is my response to your letter about my memories of the day
President Kennedy was assassinated.

The day that John F. Kennedy died, my quartet was recording in the
30th Street studios of Columbia Records. One of the sound engineers
had heard the news on the radio on the way to work. The musicians were
stunned. We stared at ech other in disbelief. The assassination so
consumed our thoughts, that we were unable to continue. The recording
session was cancelled. Driving home to Connecticut from New York City
I heard the story over and over on the car radio. At home I found my
wife and children glued to the TV set. The entire family, from the
teenagers down to the baby reacted as if the President had been one of
our family. He was the first president with whom we could identify, who
seemed close to us in age and outlook. His 'John John' was the same
age as our Matthew. We spent days mourning, and watching TV as the
horrible drama of Kennedy, Oswald and Ruby unfolded. The cortege and
the funeral were as real as if we were there. The images of Jacqueline
in the black veil, young John with the tiny flag, and the sound of taps
and the bagpipes are indelibly stamped into my memory. We had lost one
of our own. I think we subliminally knew that we were entering a new
and perhaps dangerous but certainly radically different era.

Sincerely,

Dave Brubeck

ZBIGNIEW BRZEZINSKI, *statesman, U.S. National Security Advisor*

Center for Strategic & International Studies
Georgetown University • Washington DC

July 5, 1985

Dear Mrs. Hansen:

With reference to your question, I was having
lunch at the Faculty Club at Columbia University when the waiter came up and told me and
the friend with whom I was lunching, "President
Kennedy has just been shot." I remember literally
leaping up from my chair, and then without sitting
down again I immediately proceeded downstairs,
to a large lounge, where there was a television
set. I sat and watched the television until
the awful moment when Walter Cronkite announced,
though he added the words "I repeat, I repeat
it is only an unconfirmed report," that the
President was dead.

Sincerely,

Zbigniew Brzezinski

Mrs. Jodie Elliott Hansen
Box 1031
Union City, Tennessee 38261

1800 K Street Northwest, Suite 400 • Washington DC 20006 • Telephone 202/887-0200
Cable Address: CENSTRAT TWX: 7108229583

ART BUCHWALD

1750 PENNSYLVANIA AVENUE, N.W.
SUITE 1311
WASHINGTON, D.C. 20006

TELEPHON
393-6680

8 June 1979

Dear Mrs. Hansen:

Thank you so much for your letter, but I regret I cannot help you. My doctors say I only have twenty more years to live and I wish to devote that time to things that I must do.

Sincerely,

Art Buchwald

BUCKINGHAM PALACE

1st. February 1980

Dear Mrs. Hansen,

I am commanded by The Queen to write
and thank you for your letter, but because of
Her Majesty's rules in these matters I am
afraid it is not possible for her to do as
you ask.

When I tell you of the many requests
that The Queen receives I feel sure you will
understand the reason for these rules and
that it would be most unfair to make any
exception to them.

Yours sincerely,

Susan Mussey.

Lady-in-Waiting

WILLIAM F. BUCKLEY, JR., *author and political commentator*

NATIONAL REVIEW·150 East 35th Street, New York, New York 100

Tel. 679-73

WILLIAM F. BUCKLEY, JR.
Editor

November 23, 1981

Dear Mrs. Hansen:

    I would be glad to recall what I was doing when I learned of the news of the President's assassination when you advise me that you have a contract to publish the book. I find it very hard to produce without that stimulus.

Yours faithfully,

Wm. F. Buckley, Jr.

Mrs. Jodie Elliott Hansen
Box 1031
Union City, TN   38261

GEORGE BURNS

October 30, 1979

Dear Mrs. Hansen-

"I was working in my office with my
writers when my secretary came in very whitefaced and told us the news. We immediately
turned on the television and watched in
stunned silence. None of us said much of
anything, and none of us cried. It wasn't
until hours later when I arrived home, when
Gracie and I saw each other we both burst
into tears."

Good luck with your book.

Yours truly,

George Burns
George Burns

Mrs. Jodie Elliott Hansen
Box 1031
Union City, Tenn. 38261

JAMES MACGREGOR BURNS, *historian, political scientist,*
presidential biographer

WILLIAMS COLLEGE
WILLIAMSTOWN, MASSACHUSETTS 01267

DEPARTMENT OF POLITICAL SCIEN
STETSON HA

February 27, 1984

Mrs. Jodie Elliott Hansen
Box 1031
Union City, TN 38261

Dear Mrs. Hansen:

   In answer to your query, news came to me of Kennedy's assassination
when I was teaching American government to a class in the basement of the
Congregational Church here in Williamstown; the College was short of classroom space at that time and borrowing rooms from the church. A student
came in with a report of Kennedy's being wounded; we paused a bit then
went on with the class. Some minutes later the student came back to say
that Kennedy was dead. We kept the class going, as in a trance, until we *soon*
all realized that there was no point. I went home to be with my grieving
family, only to be overwhelmed by telephone calls and by the arrival of
television interviewers.

   Best of luck in your project.

                                        Sincerely,

                                        James M Burns

                                        James MacGregor Burns

JMB/lg

BARBARA BUSH, *First Lady of the United States*

OFFICE OF THE VICE PRESIDENT

WASHINGTON

July 31, 1985

Dear Mrs. Hansen,

   Thank you very much for your recent letter to Mrs. Bush
asking for her reactions, location, etc. to the initial news of
the assassination of President John F. Kennedy on November 22,
1963.

   Mrs. Bush has written the following account:

   "At the time of the assassination of President Kennedy,
George and I were campaigning in East Texas (Tyler,
I think). George was running for the U.S. Senate.
At the moment I heard, I was having my hair done
in a new-to-me beauty shop ... getting ready to
go on to Dallas, Texas, to the <u>Crystal Ball</u> that
evening. Suddenly, I heard of the shooting over
the shop radio. Somehow or other I could not get
anyone else in the beauty parlor to stop talking
and to listen. Nobody seemed to care. I remember
the horror of it all very well. The phone rang,
and it was my husband. He said they'd be by for
me in a minute. So with damp hair I left. I <u>so</u>
wanted to be with George and especially with our
children. At that time nobody knew what had really
happened. Was the President merely wounded? Who
else had been hurt? What <u>had</u> really happened?

   We got in our campaign plane and went on to Dallas.
When we landed we heard the news and promptly took
off for Houston. George had the same reaction that
I had -- we had to be home with our children.

   As an aside: The lady who lived with us was from
Central America. She said, 'Americans are so
violent.' I was very shocked. I had thought of
Central Americans as being violent ... not North
Americans."

                    Sincerely,

                    Susan Porter Rose
                    Chief of Staff to
                    Mrs. Bush

GEORGE BUSH

710 NORTH POST OAK ROAD
SUITE 208
HOUSTON, TEXAS 77024

(713) 467-1980

August 25, 1979

Mrs. Jodie Elliott Hansen
Box 1031
Union City, TN 38261

Dear Mrs. Hansen,

Thank you for your letter of August 10.

As to your query, I was in Tyler, Texas on November 22,
1963 to give a political speech. My initial reaction
to the news that President Kennedy had been shot was
disbelief, and then a sense of horror, once I finally
realized it actually happened. That was the general
reaction of people I met that tragic day.

I have enclosed a brochure and a campaign newsletter.
I'd be most grateful if you can see fit to support my
candidacy for President.

Again, thanks for writing. Hopefully, our paths will
cross next time I'm in your area.

Sincerely,

George Bush

EARL L. BUTZ

Dean Emeritus of Agriculture

Room 586 Krannert Building

Purdue University

West Lafayette, Indiana 47907

Office 317-494-4307

317-494-4304

Home 317-743-1097

November 2, 1983

Mrs. Jodie Elliott Hansen
Box 1031
Union City, Tennessee   38261

Dear Mrs. Hansen:

When news of the Kennedy assassination flashed over the radio on that tragic day in 1963, I was lying on the davenport at home recuperating from recent surgery.

I was dumbfounded. I simply couldn't accept the fact that this could happen in My Country.

But it did!

After the initial shock, I was thankful that this was the work of a single madman. No coup was attempted, no armies marched; no attempt was made to overturn constitutional government - this all in sharp contrast to much of the rest of the world where violence and revolution are ever threatening.

How fortunate that we live in a nation where democracy prevails, even in crises.

Sincerely,

Earl L. Butz

Earl L. Butz
Dean Emeritus of Agriculture

ELB/mb

Erskine Caldwell

26 February 1983

Dear Mrs Hansen:

My wife and I were in an airline ticket office in New York when we first heard of the assassination of President Kennedy. The airline clerk was so flustered and nervous that she was unable to find the correct listing of the airline flight we wished to reserve. It was all very strange in the beginning, because she was constantly wiping tears from her eyes. Finally, she put aside her papers and began shaking her head.

"I just can't do it", she said, sobbing. "I'm sorry--I just can't do it:"

"What's the matter?" we asked

"Don't you know?" she asked.

"Know what?"

"About him--he was killed--murdered:"

"Who?"

The president--President Kennedy:"

And that was how the news of the assassination of Jokn F. Kennedy was relayed to us on that fateful day.

Sincerely,

Erskine Caldwell

P.O.Box 4550/Hopi Station
Scottsdale, Arizona 85258

LIZ CARPENTER, *journalist, aide to President Lyndon Johnson*

The day – Nov. 22, 1963 – will always bring a shudder and a chill for I was there in Dallas, in the motorcade, and, as executive assistant to the man who must take over – LBJ – my memory is jarred by the wave of emotion: disbelief, then horror, then the long ride back on air force one and the pride that

so many Americans from Photographer Cecil Stoughton to the new President himself rose to the occasion and lifted this country to Continuity. I drafted the words he spoke on arriving in Washington but really God drafted them. Some greater power saw us all through –

Liz Carpenter

December 14, 1979

Mrs. Jodie Elliott Hansen
Box 1031
Union City, Tennessee 38261

Dear Mrs. Hansen:

In response to your letter of Nov 19th, here is a brief account of my memories of the day when the late President John F. Kennedy was assassinated.

> "I was in my office at 498 7th Ave., when
> as assistant nofified me that President
> Kennedy had been shot. I know I was
> transfixed until later on when the news
> that he had died came through. Then I closed
> myself in my office and cried."

Thank you for including my comments in your book.

Sincerely,

OLEG CASSINI

OC/amg

WILLIAM B. CATTON, *historian*

Otterside Cond. C-2
Middlebury, Vt.05753
January 15, 1980

Mrs. Jodie Elliott Hansen
Box 1031
Union City, Tennessee 38261

Dear Mrs. Hansen:

Your letter to my father of last November 10 was just forwarded to me (along with an accumulation of other mail)
by Doubleday & Company.

I regret to say that my father died in August 1978 after
a brief illness.

You may have learned about this since writing him, but
I wanted to make some sort of response lest you form
the impression that he was simply ignoring your interesting request. He was always very good about replying
promptly, and I'm sure he would have found time to send
you a few paragraphs for your book.

In fact, he and I were together -- having martinis in the
bar at the Algonquin Hotel in New York -- when the first
news of Kennedy's assassination began to come in over the
radio. We were appalled, and we spent the next couple of
hours alternately making sorrowful comments and listening
anxiously for more news. The entire bar and restaurant at
the Algonquin became a hushed and sober place as people
with portable radios heard and passed along the various
bulletins.

You have heard from some interesting and impressive people
already, and I believe your project is a good one. The very
best of luck with it. I wish that my father could be here
to respond directly.

Sincerely,

William B. Catton
Professor of History
Middlebury College

ALFRED D. CHANDLER, *Pulitzer Prize–winning professor of business history at Harvard Business School and Johns Hopkins University*

HARVARD UNIVERSITY

GRADUATE SCHOOL OF BUSINESS ADMINISTRATION

GEORGE F. BAKER FOUNDATION

ALFRED D. CHANDLER, JR.
Straus Professor of Business History

SOLDIERS FIELD
BOSTON, MASSACHUSETTS 02163

February 19, 1980

Mrs. Jodie Elliott Hansen
Box 1031
Union City, TN 38261

Dear Mrs. Hansen:

I'm happy to respond to your request about where I was and my reactions to the assassination of President Kennedy.

I was at that time a Professor of History at Johns Hopkins where I was editing the papers of Dwight D. Eisenhower. I had gone to Wilmington to do research for a biography I was then writing of Pierre S. du Pont. As I boarded the train in Wilmington for Baltimore, I noticed a woman crying and then saw others doing the same. I was then told that the President had been shot. I was particularly stunned as I had been a classmate of Jack Kennedy's at Harvard and we had sailed together on the Harvard sailing team. That evening I had dinner with Milton Eisenhower, Ike's brother, who was then the President of Johns Hopkins and several of the close associates of the two Eisenhowers. We watched the news and talked at length about its implications. As a historian I do feel that the assassination marked an important turning point in American history. Since that day the Presidency has not enjoyed the prestige and to use a more current term, the credibility had for the 30 years since Franklin Roosevelt took office been so important to the nation's performance at home and abroad.

I hope these comments have some value to you.

Sincerely,

Alfred D. Chandler

Alfred D. Chandler, Jr.

ADC/abh

JOHN CHAPPELL *(in 1963) student at Southeastern Baptist Theological Seminary, North Carolina*

I had worked for JFK when he was campaigning for President. I worked with the Young Democrats at Wake Forest where I was a student at the time. I was also a member of a group—probably the smallest group supporting him in the whole country. It was called "Baptists for Kennedy" and there were about 8 members. We were a little ticked off by the prejudice and the issues being raised about Kennedy's being a Catholic, as if that would make any difference....When Kennedy came to Raleigh, all 8 of us went to hear him speak. We had our signs and our big banner we had painted that said, "Southern Baptists for Kennedy." When the Kennedy campaign workers saw us with our signs, they gave us good seats in the coliseum. The cameras were focused so that every time they had a front view of the Senator our banner was right behind his head and there on television was "Southern Baptists for Kennedy." After his speech, someone tugged his sleeve. He turned around and saw the sign and grinned. So we all went down on the platform and met him....(Upon hearing the assassination news) we all rushed to the nearest television set and I remember seeing Walter Cronkite in his shirt sleeves, a sight we all remember, how he was obviously shaken and upset. I felt a personal loss at this death.

THE FRENCH CHEF
WGBH-TV, CHANNEL 2
BOSTON, MASSACHUSETTS 02134

15 September 1981

Mrs. Jodie Hansen
Box 1031
Union City, Tennessee   38261

Dear Mrs. Hansen,

     I certainly remember very vividly, as I suppose every
one around at that tragic time does, exactly where we were
when we heard the news of JFK's assassination. We were sitting
in our kitchen and were about to have lunch, a friend called
up and said, "Turn on the television,Kennedy has been shot!"
We turned it on, just as the cortege was arriving at the
Parkland Hospital. Like most people I know, we never turned
it off until the funeral was over. Because we saw every
minute of everything we have never had the slightest doubts
that it was Oswald and Oswald alone who shot the President.
We heard all about his movements and the shooting of Officer
Tippet, and finally his capture, and we saw him being shot by
Ruby. I think people who didn't experience all of that are
probably prone to the conspiracy theory, because they really
hadn't participated in what was going on, like the finding of
the rifle, the finding of the mail order to A. Hiddell, of
the pistol that shot Officer Tippet, and so forth and so on.
That was certainly a time we shall never forget and it still
fills us with horror and sorrow.

     Good luck on your book. It will be very interesting
to read.

Yours sincerely,

Mrs. Paul Child   *Julia Child*

FRANK CHURCH, *U.S. Senator from Idaho*

WHITMAN & RANSOM

1333 NEW HAMPSHIRE AVE., N.W.

WASHINGTON, D.C. 20036

522 FIFTH AVENUE
NEW YORK, N.Y. 10036
212-575-5800

5 SOUTH FLOWER STREET
LOS ANGELES, CA 90071
213-485-1080

289 GREENWICH AVENUE
GREENWICH, CONNECTICUT 06830
203-869-3800

3 LANDMARK SQUARE
STAMFORD, CONNECTICUT 06901
203-356-1130

202-785-1600
CABLE: WHITSOM, D.C.

December 18, 1981

Mrs. Jodie Elliott Hansen
Box 1031
Union City, Tennessee 38261

Dear Mrs. Hansen:

In response to your letter of November 18, 1981, asking for a personal account of what I was doing, the reaction of others around me, and how they first heard the news of the assassination of President John F. Kennedy, this is my personal recollection.

I was attending a lunch in the Secretary's private dining room at the State Department, in the company of several other Senators and departmental officials. The door was flung open by a staff assistant who announced that "The President has been shot in Texas!"

I remember that the Senators immediately dispersed. One of them, Senator John Sparkman as I recall, attempted to get through to the White House by phone but found all the circuits busy. I put a call through to my office, where the news of the tragedy was confirmed by my press secretary.

I then drove back to the Capitol, where the Senate was called into emergency session and the official confirmation of the President's death was received.

I hope this account will serve your purposes.

Sincerely,

Frank Church

CRAIG CLAIBORNE

July 27, 1981

Jodie Elliot Hansen
Box 1031
Union City, Tennessee   38261

Dear Mrs. Hansen:

I vividly recall the day of John F. Kennedy's assassination. I
had dined at mid-day in a West Side restaurant. I was escorting
a young lady back to work and, when we paused for a stop light at
a corner on Fifth Avenue, we noticed the crowds in front of and
inside St. Patrick's Cathedral. A policeman standing near the corner
was sobbing and he composed himself long enough to tell us of the
tragedy. It was, of course, a stunning moment and we walked away
in grief and silence.

Yours truly,

MARK W. CLARK, *U.S. Army General; president, The Citadel Military College*

Full Name ___Gen. Mark Wayne Clark_____ Age _83_____

Current Address ___17 Country Club Dr._____ Address Nov. '63 The Citadel,
___Charleston, S. C. 29412___ ___Charleston, S. C. 29409___
Occupation or Profession now _Retired. I am president emeritus of The Citadel and chairman,_
Occupation or Profession Nov. '63 _President, The Citadel_ American Battle Monuments Commission

Use space below and please include small details, such as: if you saved any
newspaper clippings or memorial publications; if you had ever seen or met
President Kennedy; if you (at the time) were worried or apprehensive about
the possibility of a world crisis or a conspiracy; if your community had any
special church or memorial services, etc. Any small detail is important.

I heard of the tragic news of President Kennedy's assassination while in an automobile
en route to address a student body of a high school in Atlanta, Ga. I remember how
shocked and distressed I was and that I started my remarks to the student body, gathered
in assembly, by stating that it was my sad duty to relay to them some very disheartening
news. Then I proceeded to tell them about the death of the President.

When I returned to The Citadel the next day, I learned that I had received a message
from the Royal (British) Navy Staff in Washington telling me to half staff as a
mark of respect the White Ensign of the Royal Navy which flies at The Citadel. That
ensign flies alongside the Stars and Stripes over a monument on The Citadel campus
which commemorates the World War II cooperation of the two nations of America and
Great Britain. The monument is comprised of relics salvaged from the famous submarine
which served as the HMS Seraph and the U.S.S. Seraph. As it happened, my career was
associated with some of the Seraph's important missions. I was therefore naturally
pleased when officials of the two nations decided to sponsor erecting on The Citadel
campus a monument that perpetuates the memory of this great vessel.

I am attaching brief information about the Seraph Monument.

ARTHUR C. CLARK, *science fiction author*

From: **ARTHUR C. CLARKE**

As I now receive <u>thousands</u> of items of mail a year - which often takes many months to reach Sri Lanka - it is impossible for me to answer letters personally. This reply is designed to deal with 90% of the questions I am asked. I hope you will understand the need for it, and thank you for your interest.

Address: "Leslie's House", 25, Barnes Place, Colombo 7, Sri Lanka.
Telephones: Colombo 94255: 598730: 94012.
Telegraph: UNDERSEA, Colombo, Sri Lanka.
U.K. Office: Rocket Publishing Company, Dene Court, Bishop's
Lydeard, TA4 3LT, England **Telephone:-** (0)823 432 671

Biography: see WHO'S WHO, CONTEMPORARY AUTHORS, CONTEMPORARY NOVELISTS, DICTIONARY OF INTERNATIONAL BIOGRAPHY, CELEBRITY REGISTER, BRITTANICA 3, etc. Also: ASCENT TO ORBIT; 1984: SPRING; THE TREASURE OF THE GREAT REEF; THE VIEW FROM SERENDIP.

Bibliography: Now about 60 books. See above refs., also AGAINST THE NIGHT, THE STARS (J. Hollow; Harcourt, Brace Jovanovich) and ARTHUR C CLARKE: A Primary & Secondary Bibliography (D. Samuelson; G.K. Hall).

Rights: I no longer accept commissions of **any** kind; queries concerning my published works should be addressed to:-
David Higham Associates, 5-8 Lower John Street, Golden Square, London, WIR 4HA, England. **Telephone:** 437 7778.
or Scott Meredith, 845, Third Avenue, New York, N.Y. 10022, U.S.A. **Telephone:** 245 5500.

Lectures: I am no longer able to accept lecture requests, even **inside** Sri Lanka. The demands on my time make it utterly impossible, but there's another reason. I will no longer attend functions (private or public) where smoking is permitted. This has greatly simplified my life (and, I hope, prolonged it.)

Space: There are literally hundreds of books and magazines readily available on this enormous subject, and numerous organisations dealing with it at all levels from popular to professional. Specimen copies of its publications can be obtained from The British Interplanetary Society at 27 S. Lambeth Rd., London, SW8 1SZ

Photos: Sorry, but I cannot autograph and mail back books; (it sometimes takes hours to clear them through local Customs!)

Manuscripts: UNDER NO CIRCUMSTANCES will I comment on MSS or story ideas. (See the essay "Dear Sir...." in VOICES FROM THE SKY for a few reasons.) And to all those enthusiasts who send me pet theories, inventions, and plans for saving the human race - I'm sorry, but I have neither the time nor the qualifications to comment.

Advice to Authors: The only advice I can give to would-be authors is as follows: Read at least one book a day, and write as much as you can. Study the memoirs of authors who interest you. (Somerset Maugham's A WRITER'S NOTEBOOKS is a good example.) Correspondence courses, writer's schools, etc., are probably useful - but all the authors I know were self-taught. There is no substitute for living; as Hemingway wisely remarked, "Writing is not a full-time occupation".

2001: The answer to all queries on this subject will be found in the novels 2001: A SPACE ODYSSEY (NAL in U.S., Corgi in U.K.) and 2010: ODYSSEY TWO (Del Rey in U.S., Granada in U.K.) See also THE LOST WORLDS OF 2001 (NAL in U.S., Sidgwick & Jackson in U.K.) and REPORT ON PLANET THREE (Harper & Row, U.S.: Gollancz, U.K.) Jerome Agel's THE MAKING OF KUBRICK'S 2001 (NAL) is also a very useful reference, with many photos. (Oh yes - I've promised (?) to deliver ODYSSEY THREE on New Year's Eve, 2000.)

Publicity Quotes: So many publishers and authors have asked me to comment on books, or to write prefaces, that I am now forced to turn down all such requests, no matter how good the cause.

Requests for help: If I responded to all the appeals I get for literary, financial, educational, etc. assistance I would have no time (or money) for anything else. It is often difficult to ignore genuine and deserving cases, but I salve my conscience with the thought that I now directly support about 50 people.

University of Moratuwa: As the Chancellor is in no way involved in administration, please write directly to the University on all matters concerning appointments, admissions, etc.

The Arthur Clarke Centre: As above. Please write to the Director.

Interviews: I am always willing to see visitors, but please phone in advance. However, I no longer give interviews as (a) I've done several **thousand** in the last forty years and the boredom is now excruciating (b) everything I want to say is in my books.

This is v. strange - I can't even remember what country I was in!! Yet I was certainly v. upset. And I have clear memories of the A-bomb & Pearl Harbor!

Sorry - Arthur C Clarke

1 Nov 84

Arthur C Clarke

WILLIAM JOHN CLYDE *(in 1963) seven years old, living in Australia; later formed the Australian Kennedy Society to publicize the questions surrounding JFK's death*

Since I was only 7 years old at the time, my memories of the assassination are virtually nonexistent. I do remember asking my father why he was putting away a newspaper about the event. I remember him saying that in the future I could look back and say I "knew" the man, and I replied that I couldn't because I didn't know him. From what I have since learnt, Australians were deeply shocked by the assassination. I know of two memorials to the late President. One is a chapel high in the Australian Alps, and the other is a memorial stone and bust in one of Melbourne's foremost pubic parks. It may seem a rather small point, but for many Australians, JFK's invitation to a former Australian coastwatcher to visit the White House was a great gesture, and it was played up here at the time. You may recall the coastwatcher's small part after the PT 109 had been sunk.

JEAN ALTFELD COHEN *(in 1963) military wife living in Poitiers, France*

It almost seemed that we, Americans in exile, needed to be with one another. I did not sense the anxiety that seemed to pervade military personnel at the time of the Berlin Crisis early in the Kennedy administration. Then, we dependents particularly feared war with evacuation from the country. That evening it was more a sense of disbelief—some of which was magnified by the distance from the event. We were spared the television coverage, except for the few who had French televisions. The French mourned with us. This was evident to me when I took our three-year-old to nursery school. The French nuns had tears in their eyes and took great pains in French to express their sorrow and their horror. Jackie had captured the French totally and her sorrow and loss was theirs...Throughout the three years we were in France, I remained fascinated by the French resentment and even dislike of Americans. In Poitiers, I sensed their "Yankee go home." Yet it seemed that somehow Kennedy might reverse their plans to really send our military home. His death appeared to result in their total disenchantment with us. Somehow Johnson and his chili could not replace Kennedy and his cuisine. Thus his demise marked the end of an American-French era. I often wondered what might have been if Kennedy had lived.

BELLERIVE
ST. PETER
BARBADOS, WEST INDIES

Dear Mrs. Hansen —
    In November - 1963 - I was appearing on Broadway in "The Irregular Verb to Love" (an English comedy) I remember I was reading in bed - my Barbadian maid had just gone marketing when she suddenly burst into my room saying the elevator operator had told her President Kennedy had been shot —) thought she had misunderstood — it was so preposterous — and unbelievable —— I jumped up + rushed to the T.V set — alas — it was indeed the horrible truth — We did not play that night and

(continued)

I believe Broadway was dark
for several nights — I'm not
certain how many performances
we cancelled.

I am sure your book will
be most interesting —
All my best wishes

Janette Cole

Monday 29 June —

WILLIAM COLBY, *CIA director*

William E. Colby
1111 19TH STREET, N. W.
WASHINGTON, D. C. 20036

(202)828-0100

July 22, 1982

Mrs. Jodie Elliott Hansen
Box 1031
Union City, Tennessee   38261

Dear Ms. Hansen:

          Thank you for your note of July 2 inviting me
to comment on the circumstances in which I heard the news
of the assassination of President Kennedy. Most people of
my vintage have a clear memory of two major events, the
news of Pearl Harbor and the news of President Kennedy's
death, and I congratulate you for your project of compiling
these experiences.

          In my own case, the news came while I was work-
ing as Chief of the Far East Division of CIA, in its headquarters in Langley, Virginia. I had been heavily involved
with President Kennedy and his advisors over the previous
months in discussions about our Vietnam policy. Despite
some differences with some of his staff, I had the highest
respect for President Kennedy's efforts to carry on the
torch passed to his "new generation" of which I felt a part.
On first hearing the news, my comment was that this would
make a major change in the future of our country and even
of the world which had been so captivated by his personality
and leadership. I felt a great sense of sadness at the op-
portunities which would be lost by the absence of his charis-
matic leadership and a disappointment that his potential had
been cut down so much before his time.

          With all best regards.

                              Sincerely,

                              W.E. Colby

WEC:pdk

ARCHIMEDES CONCON *(in 1963) physician living in Quezon City, Philippines*

I was going to a breakfast meeting at the Wak Wak Golf and Country Club in Mandaluyong, Rizal, in the suburbs of Manila. We got the news of President John F. Kennedy's assassination over the radio at 9 a.m., Manila time. As I remember it, the people at the meeting took the news calmly and went on with the business at hand as if nothing had happened. Generally speaking, the Filipino people in common with other East Asians can take tragic news with sangfroid. We do not show our emotions to the rest of the world. We would rather keep it within ourselves. Those who grieved President John F. Kennedy's tragic death did it silently in secret in the innermost chambers of their hearts.

SERGIU COMISSIONA *(in 1963) director of the Haifa symphony*

I was giving a party in my apartment in Haifa, Israel. Everyone was having a good time and my guests were talking and laughing as they looked out over the lights of the harbor. It was a beautiful evening. Suddenly the music was interrupted by an announcement of President Kennedy's death. The party was hushed. Below, the street filled with people. Groups congregated on street corners talking in undertones. It was as if war had broken out....I felt that one era had ended, and a new era had begun. For me, the Twentieth Century ended on November 21, 1963.

JOHN B. CONNALLY, *Governor of Texas, rode with President Kennedy in the Dallas motorcade*

CONNALLY
LEADERSHIP FOR AMERICA

May 7, 1979

Mrs. Jodie Hansen
P. O. Box 1031
Union City, Tennessee   38261

Dear Mrs. Hansen:

      I appreciate your most interesting letter relating the many recollections regarding November 22, 1963.

      Nellie and I do not often talk about that dramatic event, although we did vividly recount the incident in the recent House Committee hearing.

      Our memories, as you can understand, are such that we prefer not to dwell on a very tragic day.

Sincerely,

John Connally

John B. Connally

JBC:nw

Connally for President Headquarters
Post Office Box 8236, Washington, D.C. 20024
3110 Columbia Pike, Arlington, Virginia
Telephone: (703) 892-5500

Houston Office
711 Polk St., Suite 601, Houston, Texas 77002
Telephone: (713) 651-0000

Paid for by Connally for President Committee. A copy of our report is filed with the Federal Election Commission and is available for purchase from the Federal Election Commission, Washington, D.C.

A. DENTON COOLEY, M.D., *surgeon, performed first artificial heart transplant*

CARDIOVASCULAR ASSOCIATES
TEXAS HEART INSTITUTE
P. O. BOX 20345   HOUSTON, TEXAS 77025

Surgery

September 18, 1981

Mrs. Jodie Elliott Hansen
Box 1031
Union City, Tennessee   38261

Dear Mrs. Hansen:

What do I recall about the news of John Kennedy's assassination? On the day of his assassination when the news broke, we were operating in the Texas Heart Institute of St. Luke's and Texas Children's Hospital. It is our custom to play the radio during the day so that we can hear music, but also keep abreast of the news. Had we not had this policy, we would not have known of the event for perhaps several hours.

I recall that the heart was open and that the pump oxygenator or that cardiopulmonary bypass was functioning. When this news came over the radio, we were all aghast. While it was necessary to continue on with the operation, we all remained perfectly silent each with his own thoughts trying to comprehend the importance of this event and the influence it would have upon our country.

From that moment on and throughout the rest of the day, there was no jocularity or our usual light conversation. Each member of my staff was as deeply concerned as I.

Fortunately, the operation which we were performing turned out well and we went on to more similar procedures before that day was over. I was anxious to get home to discuss this situation with my children. My wife was deeply grieved and acted as though she had lost a close member of her own family.

I hope this information may be of some use to you. With best wishes for success of your book, I am

Yours sincerely,

Denton A. Cooley, M.D.

DAC:jm

NORMAN COUSINS, *political journalist, world peace advocate*

UNIVERSITY OF CALIFORNIA, LOS ANGELES   UCLA

BERKELEY · DAVIS · IRVINE · LOS ANGELES · RIVERSIDE · SAN DIEGO · SAN FRANCISCO   SANTA BARBARA · SANTA CRUZ

DEPARTMENT OF PSYCHIATRY AND
BIOBEHAVIORAL SCIENCES
ADDRESS REPLIES TO:
RM. 2859 SLICHTER HALL
LOS ANGELES, CALIFORNIA 90024

August 19, 1983

Mrs. Jodie Elliott Hansen
Box 1031
Union City, Tennessee   38261

Dear Mrs. Hansen,

At the time of the President's assassination, I was on the Merritt Parkway,
driving from my home in New Canaan, Connecticut, to my office in New
York. When I turned on the car radio, I heard the news announcer saying
something about a bullet striking the Governor of Texas. Then he said
that there were unsubstantiated reports about the President having been
hit by a ricocheting bullet but the announcer explained that these reports
were unconfirmed. I switched to another station, my mind not yet fully
grasping the possibilities. This time the news announcer, his voice
far more excitable and ominous, was saying something about the President's
car being diverted to the hospital because the President was wounded but
that there was no indication that the wound was serious. I pulled the
car over to the side of the road and sat mute and stunned as word by
word and minute by minute the tragedy unfolded. For 90 minutes or more
I sat there listening to fragmentary but mind-shattering accounts, still
unable to comprehend fully what was happening. But the fragments kept
coming, each more ominous than the last, and I could no longer keep from
myself the reality that John F. Kennedy, who was on his way to becoming
a great President and whom I was proud to know as a personal friend, had
been shot in the head and might not be able to survive. Finally, the
culminating news announcement came over the radio and I rested my head
on the steering wheel. How long I sat this way on the side of the road
I can't recall. I do remember thinking that the loss was not just to
the American people but to Englishmen and Russians and Italians and
Chinese and Japanese and everyone else, for he had embarked on a course
designed to reduce the tensions among nations and to lessen the dangers
of a war that could set fire to the world, like a torch being set to
a bird's nest. That terrible feeling has never left me. Indeed, it has
a fiercer reality today than ever before.

                    Sincerely,

                    Norman Cousins

NC/cpb

GILES M. CROUCH *(in 1963) U.S. Navy seaman stationed in Groton, Connecticut, following service in the U.S. Naval Ceremonial Honor Guard in Washington during which he witnessed the President greet hundreds of visiting dignitaries*

That morning I had read in the papers about President Kennedy's Texas trip and I had been listening to the radio and heard the remark the President had made about Mrs. Kennedy's being late for one of their appearances, but always looked prettier than he—or something to that effect. I and the others in the barracks turned on the TV set and while sitting there in my dress uniform with my bag beside me, I heard the report of the President's death. I will never forget the feeling I had. I felt absolutely worthless as a human being. My whole mind and body seemed to stop functioning. I remember having this heavy burden of pain which was overwhelming. I had not, at that time, experienced the death of anyone close to me—not even a grandparent. JFK was my hero.

<hr>

JOHN DEBETENCOURT *(in 1963) living in Belgium*

The first impression of a foreign country was to wonder how this would affect the world and if the political world situation would be jeopardized by his death.... Such violence can occur in every country. We had the opinion that this act of violence can happen more often in your country where anyone can buy a weapon without any problems. It was not such a strange fact that your President could be killed.

OLIVIA DE HAVILLAND, *Oscar-winning actress*

Paris, France

January 27, 1982

Dear Jodie Hansen,

For reasons I won't explain here, your kind letter of many, many months ago has only just come into my hands.

I'm so sorry about the delay in this reply, and hope that it does not reach you too late to be of help.

Your letter asks me to write you, as a contribution to the book you are compiling, a recollection of the moment when I first heard the news of President Kennedy's assassination. Here it is:

I was here in Paris when the assassination occurred, and learned of it in the evening, Paris time, through a friend who phoned me with the news. The following morning I had the difficult task of telling my daughter, then a child of seven, about this tragic happening. Above her bed hung a photograph of President Kennedy, Mrs. Kennedy, and their children, sent to my daughter by a good friend who knew of Gisèle's keen admiration of the President. And so, after she had awakened and was still in bed, with the photo of the beloved idol above her, I gave her the news as gently and calmly as I could. It seemed better for me to tell her in this way than for her to learn of it through the radio or from an over-wrought friend.

As for me, the whole world seemed to change that day. The unthinkable had happened. Alas, it has been happening ever since.

Again, my apologies for the tardiness of this reply, and with every good wish,

Most sincerely,

Olivia de Havilland

Mrs. Jodie Elliott Hansen
Box 1031
803 E. Exchange Street
Union City, Tennessee 38261

Phyllis Diller

My agent in New York called me in St. Louis
to tell me President Kennedy had been shot
in Dallas. I was shocked and upset. I was
in the middle of an engagement at the Crystal
Palace. I called the owner Jay Landesman and
told him it would be impossible for me to go
on that night and do comedy. I didn't think
anyone would come out anyway. He understood
and therefore the theatre was dark that night
as was the mood of the entire world.

- Phyllis Diller

June 1982

ROBERT DOMBROSKI *(in 1963) network switchman,*
New Jersey Telephone & Telegraph Company

At the time President Kennedy was shot, I was working in the central office.
Our office went into an overload condition, faster than I had ever seen. There
were 22 of us in the office, all trying to find a trouble condition that would put
us into the overload. A call came in from my wife who told me that Kennedy
was shot. She had the radio at home, tuned in to the news. As we were not
allowed, at that time, to have a radio I asked her to put the phone near the
radio. I then put the call on the office intercom for all to hear the news. The
reaction of the men I worked with was mixed. One fellow, a member of the
John Birch Society, said, "It's about time someone killed that nigger loving
bastard." A young fellow said, "Shit, I bet it's a damn war going to start
and I'll get drafted. Christ! My wife is going to have a baby. What the hell
do the communists want now?" Another fellow said that his wife was in love
with Kennedy and this news would kill her. About that time one of the other
guys ran into the maintenance center and said there was a fight outside. We
all rushed to the front door to see. Two police officers were holding two men
apart and one of the men was hollering "That bastard said he was glad Ken-
nedy was shot." Then a woman in a car stopped in the street and said that
Kennedy was still alive. The crowd all cheered, and the police let both men
go and told them to go to church and pray for Kennedy.

ANTAL DORATI, *conductor and composer*

Antal Dorati
Detroit Symphony Orchestra
Ford Auditorium   Detroit, Michigan 48226

March 26, 1980

Mrs. Jodie Elliott Hansen
Box 1031
Union City, Tennessee, 38261

Dear Mrs. Hansen:

Thank you for your letter of 6 March.

I remember well the day of the assassination of President
Kennedy. I was rehearsing in London with the BBC Symphony
Orchestra, of which I was then chief conductor.

The news arrived at intermission. I was told about the
tragic incident by the members of the orchestra who rushed
to my dressing room. I turned on the radio and heard the
account of what had happened. I tried to continue our work
but neither I or the orchestra members were able to go on.
We were too much under the shock.

Subsequently I went to the American Embassy at Grosevnor
Square and sat with my friends, numbed, trying to make sense
of the jumbled news reports which came over the wireless.

I trust this will be of help with your book.

With best wishes,

[signature]

ALLEN DRURY

May 25, 1982

Dear Mrs. Hansen,

I was in the midele of a lecture to the Women's Club of Louisville, Ky., when the chairwoman interrupted with the news flash of the shooting of the President. We did not know then what had happened, of course, and the first report was generally optimistic--or in the desperate hopes of the rustling audience, at least, was optimistic. I left, still not knowing the outcome, and started driving down the freeway toward Florida, where I was going for a time. About as I was getting on the freeway the flash came that the President had died. I remember crying for a couple of minutes, not so much for Jack Kennedy, whom I had known on the Hill as a relatively lightweight Senator and later as a relatively lightweight ~~President,~~ President, but just for America, whose promise is still so bright and yet where such terrible things can happen. What happened a year ago with ~~Reagan~~ Reagan was a sad reprise, bringing it all back with instantaneous vividness.

Best regards,

Allen Drury

Robert L. DuPont, M.D., P.A.

Psychiatry

Behavioral Health

September 15, 1981

Mrs. Jodie Elliott Hansen
Box 1031
Union City, Tennessee 38261

Dear Mrs. Hansen:

I was an intern at the Cleveland City Hospital
when I heard that President Kennedy had been shot.
A patient I saw in the clinic brought the news to
me. I had been close to this patient because he was
a young man felled by a heart attack and I had worked
with him through many sleepless nights (for both of
us) following his admission. He was returning that
day for his first outpatient visit after discharge
from the hospital. Somehow his bringing the tragic
news and sharing my shock deepened even further our
bond.

Later, when I returned to my apartment, I spent
the weekend, when not working at the hospital, glued
to the television feeling sad, confused and vulnerable.
In some way I think of that weekend as a time of
growing up for me. A sad realization of the importance
and the fragility of leadership, but also the realization that life goes on (at both a personal and a
political level) and that outcomes are often surprising.

John Kennedy, it now seems to me, did more for
the country through his death than he was ever likely
to have done as a living politician. I guess that adds
up to a bit of humility and wonder about the strange
ways that life works.

Sincerely,

Robert L. DuPont, M.D.

cr

6191 Executive Blvd.   Rockville, Maryland 20852   (301) 468-8980

JAMES H. EDMONSON *(in 1963) worked for WBRZ in Baton Rouge, Louisiana*

I will never forget how the news was announced to the viewers that day. We received it over the wire service while there was a live local news and variety-type show in progress with Walter Hill and his female co-hostess interviewing a guest. Another announcer ran into the newsroom, waving his arms around, grabbed the sheet of paper with the news report on it, and ran right in front of the camera, grabbed the microphone and in a shaky, emotional voice, announced that the President had been shot in Dallas. He then ran back out of sight. Walter Hill picked up the sheet of paper, looked at it, and said that this report was apparently true. He then said, "What do you say to something like this? We'll have to cut to something—a commercial or something—I don't know what to say."

DAVID MAX EICHORN, *rabbi*

RABBI DAVID MAX EICHHORN, D.D., D.H.L.

September 1 to April 15

311 Somerset Arms Apts.
Satellite Beach, Fla. 32935
Ph. (305) 262-2076

Rabbi David Max Eichhorn
Box 2629
Satellite Beach
Florida 32937

April 15 to September 1

85-14 66th Avenue
Rego Park, N.Y. 11374
Ph. (212) IL 9-2729 or TW 6-7147

On Friday, November 22, 1963, I was at the American air base at West Ruislip, England. I had been sent to Europe by the U.S. Air Force to conduct spiritual retreats for Jewish personnel stationed at American air bases in Turkey, Spain, Germany, France and England. This was part of my official responsibilities in the position I held at that time, that of Director of Field Operations of the Commission on Jewish Chaplaincy of the National Jewish Welfare Board. On this trip I was accompanied by my wife. This was the last stop on our Air Force assignment. XXXXXXXXXXXXXXXXXXXXXXXXXXXXXXXXXXXXX

In the late afternoon of that Friday, my wife and I were sitting in the office of the Jewish chaplain stationed at West Ruislip discussing with him the evening's Sabbath service which he would conduct and at which I would speak. As we were talking, the chaplain's wife rushed into the office with tears streaming down her face. Our first thought was that she had come to ask to be rushed to the hospital because she was in a very late stage of pregnancy. Instead she stunned us with the information that the President had been shot. About an hour later the sad news reached us that the President was dead.

The Catholic chaplain hastily arranged for an appropriate mass to be held at the Base Chapel at 2000 hours or eight p.m. After this mass was concluded, personnel of the Jewish faith gathered in the chapel for our own Sabbath service. We had planned for a lively and carefree session, with a cultural and intellectual give-and-take, and a social hour at which such Jewish goodies as gefillte fish and salami sandwiches would be served. But there was no conviviality, no give-and-take, no serving of Jewish goodies. We just held our service and then those present returned to their quarters. It was a night of sadness. Our hearts were heavy. Each felt not only that our country had lost a great leader that that he or she had suffered the loss of a gallant and warm-hearted friend.

I was traveling on military orders but my wife was not. So the next day she departed for the States on a commercial plane. Seated next to her on the homeward journey was Prince Radzewill, who was married to the President's sister and was en route to Washington to attend the President's funeral.

On this same day the West Ruislip Jewish spiritual retreat was concluded. I returned to the United States on Sunday, November 24, by military aircraft.

DAVID ERWIN *(in 1963) in boot camp training in Fort Jackson, South Carolina*

I was on the rifle range when a colonel drove up in a jeep, stepped onto the tower, and told us the news. I was stunned then, but double-stunned when the platoon sergeant stepped up to the loud speaker after the colonel had left and said, "Well they finally got Madame Nhu's lover, didn't they?" I thought at the time that the sergeant was either very insensitive and stupid or had lots of guts to stand in front of 100 or more men with loaded rifles, men who had been intensely indoctrinated with patriotism and respect for our country's leader as part of the training of boot camp and make such a callous remark. I and most of the others were very offended.

DR. ROGELIO ESCARCEGA *(in 1963) resident of Mexico*

The Mexican people felt a unique warmth and affection for JFK and his wife, and they were extremely emotional and intense in their grief for his death. I remember the tumultuous welcome and dramatic reception the President received when visiting my country a few months prior to his death. There were 3 million people on the streets and they were absolutely wild in their excitement for this opportunity to see him. There was a continuous line of people jammed on the streets—7 miles of people—as the presidential limousine drove from the airport to the Government Palace. Because the country is overwhelmingly Catholic, his attending Mass with the thousands of people at Guadalupe Shrine seemed to touch the Mexican people more than anything he could have done.

September 26, 1979

Mrs. Jodie Elliott Hansen
Box 1031
803 East Exchange Street
Union City, Tennessee 38261

Dear Mrs. Hansen:

Thank you for your letter of September 7 and I'm sure
your book will prove to be a most interesting one. As
to my own reaction to the news of President Kennedy's
assassination, I can only say it was probably much like
many others; terrible, inexpressable shock and incredibility. I happened to be on a brief visit to London
and was due to meet my older daughter and take her to
dinner and the theatre. The news, of course, canceled
all plans for everything. And, as the President and
his family had been long personal friends of my wife's
and mine, our personal horror was conceivably more
intense than most. We, of course, cabled and/or telephoned other members of the family as soon as possible
and the London Evening News asked me to write an article
about the President inasmuch as I had been a personal
friend. I sat up all night and most of the next day
with messages coming from the paper every couple of hours
to find out if my article had been completed. Everytime
I started to write something, I felt that nothing I
could say could possibly compete with others, who are more
eloquent than I, were already writing. Also, everything
I put down seemed to me a dreary and highly inaccurate
cliché. Eventually, about 24 hours later I did get out
an article which apparently satisfied the editor and it
received wide circulation and created surprisingly
favorable comment.

Sincerely,

Douglas Fairbanks, Jr.

LORETTA FERGUSON *(in 1963) housewife living in Ridgely, Tennessee*

I lost my infant son in May of 1963. He was born with the same lung con-dition as their (the Kennedy's) newborn son. I was so upset with the doctors and the hospital for not saving my baby, but after the rich and powerful Kennedys lost theirs, I realized my doctors had truly done all they could for mine and I felt less bitterness about it. I'll never forget the sad feeling and the numb sensation I had when hearing the news of the President's death.

———

JAMES FIXX *(in 1963) editor at* The Saturday Review; *later wrote the bestselling* The Complete Book of Running

I was in Rockefeller Center, just having lunch with a friend. I saw a crowd gathered around the AP machine that at that time was on display in the ground-floor window of the Associated Press Building. Someone said, "They've shot the President." In about half an hour the news wire announced that he was dead. I walked back to my office at The Saturday Review *dazed. In the elevator I met the poet John Ciardi. He had not yet heard that Kennedy was dead, so I told him. He looked at me in disbelief and then began circulat-ing on who was next in the line of succession after Johnson.*

MARY McHUGHES FERRELL *(in 1963) resident of Dallas, her husband worked for the Lincoln-Continental company that furnished automobiles for the presidential motorcade, and her personal car was borrowed to transport press*

About 12:35 p.m., I left the restaurant and walked down Elm Street toward a magazine stand at Elm and Ervay. A tall black man, with tears running down his face, stepped in front of me and asked, "Is it true they shot our President?" Momentarily, I thought he was demented. I stepped around him, but noticed, at the same time, that police vehicles were speeding down Elm toward the Triple Underpass, with riot guns held out the windows. I went to the magazine stand where small groups of people, some of them crying, were clustered around transistor radios. I again called my husband and asked if he had heard that there had been a shooting. He said he had been listening to his radio and he believed Kennedy was dead. He said there had been reports that the President had received a direct hit to the head.

CHARLOTTE FORD, *heiress, socialite, and author*

Mrs. Charlotte Ford
New York

August 4, 1982

Mrs. Jodie Elliott Hansen
P.O. Box 1031
Union City, Tennessee 38261

Dear Mrs. Hansen:

I received your letter regarding the book you are writing, which will be compiled of personal accounts from various people around the world.

I share your thoughts regarding the historical significance it will have among your readers and feel it will be quite interesting. I would therefore, be pleased to share my memories of that day with you.

I was, at the time, living in New York at the Carlyle Hotel with my mother and sister. I heard the news on the television, as I was at home in the hotel with the flu.

Our phone rang incessantly - and a close friend called and asked me to go upstairs (in the hotel) with him and console a very close friend of his who happened to be Prince Stanislaws Radziwill. I proceeded to go with my sister and try to cheer them up (he was Kennedy's brother-in-law).

I am sure your book will prove to be most promising and wish you success in your endeavor.

Sincerely,

Charlotte Ford

Charlotte Ford

CF/lb

I hope This can be of some help.

E I L E E N F O R D, *founder, Ford Models, Inc.*

FORD MODELS, INC.
344 East 59th St., New York, New York 10022
(212) 688-8538
Telex 234443 - F M A U R

February 16, 1981

Mrs. Jodie Elliott Hansen
Box 1031
Union City, Tennessee 38261

Dear Mrs. Hansen:

I am sorry to tell you that I really was not
doing anything great in November 22, 1963.
I was in Jordan Marsh selling cosmetics.(We
had our own line at the time.)

When I heard, I did not believe it and I told
all the people in the cosmetic department to
stop spreading vicious rumours and to get back
to work. The possibility of a president being
assassinated in my lifetime was totally unreal
and I still can't believe that it really
happened. It certainly signaled the beginning
of a violent stage in our history.

I wish you good luck in all your ventures.

Sincerely,

Eileen Ford

Eileen Ford

EF/sr
(Signed in Eileen Ford's absence.)

California
College
of Arts
and Crafts

5212 Broadway at College • Oakland, California 94618 • Telephone 415/653-8118

FOUNDED IN 1907

President of the College
Harry X. Ford

The day of John F. Kennedy's assasination I was at my desk at home looking over blueprints for a new College building. The radio, which had been on a music station all day suddenly interrupted its program to announce that President Kennedy had been shot. My first reaction was one of disbelief. Then before I knew it, I was on my knees crying and praying.

Later that day my wife, Celeste, returned from a short trip. She had heard the news on the car radio. We spent the rest of the afternoon together watching the news on television.

That evening while shopping at a local market, I noticed that everyone around me was in a state of shock. No one talked about the incident, nor did they wish to participate in any more conversation than was necessary.

As I was driving home, I was overwhelmed with a feeling that the assasination had marked a turning point in our lives that things would never be the same again.

Harry X. Ford
President

Accredited by the Western Association of Schools and Colleges and the National Association of Schools of Art

JOHN HOPE FRANKLIN, *Pulitzer Prize–winning historian*

Duke University
DURHAM
NORTH CAROLINA

DEPARTMENT OF HISTORY
6727 COLLEGE STATION

POSTAL CODE 27708
TELEPHONE 919—684—3626

March 7, 1983

Mrs. Jodie Elliott Hansen
Box 1031
Union City, Tennessee 38261

Dear Mrs. Hansen:

Any person who can remember as far back as November 22, 1963, has a vivid recollection of what he or she was doing when the news broke of the assassination of President John F. Kennedy. I was professor of history at Brooklyn College and chairman of the department. On that Friday afternoon, I had just left my office to begin, in the room adjoining, my honors seminar in American Studies. My secretary came in as I was chatting with students and said that my wife was calling and wished to speak to me. The first thing she said was, "This is a shock so please sit down." Then she told me that the President had been shot but she thought he was still alive and would call again when she got more information.

I returned to my fifteen students and broke the news to them. We were trying to answer the question of who and why, when a weeping student wandered into the classroom and asked aloud of anyone who could answer, "What are we going to do. He's gone." With that announcement of the President's death my students rose in a body, stood silently for a moment or two, and left the classroom. They seemed to know that I would understand; and I did.

The irony of my wife's telephoning was that I expected her to call and give me a message from the White House. On the previous day a Presidential assistant had called to inquire if I would be a member of the President's delegation to represent our country at the independence ceremonies in Zanzibar. He was to call back that Friday afternoon about that time, to give me more details and to confirm my acceptance. Needless to say I did not receive that call until Lyndon B. Johnson settled in the White House.

Sincerely yours,

John Hope Franklin

John Hope Franklin
James B. Duke Professor of History

JHF:mf

FRANK FREIDEL, *historian, presidential biographer*

HARVARD UNIVERSITY
DEPARTMENT OF HISTORY
CAMBRIDGE, MASS. 02138

ROBINSON HALL

3 December 1979

Mrs. Jodie Elliott Hansen
Box 1031
Union City, Tennessee 38261

Dear Mrs. Hansen:

You inquired where I was and what I thought when news reached me of President Kennedy's assassination. I'm sure you are receiving many interesting recollections. To all of us it was a horrible moment, never to be forgotten. In my own case, I had just come back from lunch to the offices of Elleford, Aikenoff, Inc. a firm of publishers of an American History textbook of which I am co-author. Someone said the President had been shot, and my first reaction was that it was a joke. My editor laughed and said, "Now you'll have to revise your textbook." Someone had a radio on, and we immediately learned that it was far from being a joke, and settled into a state of depression. I watched television for hours, seeing the same scenes over and over again, finding it almost impossible to accept what had happened.

With best wishes,

Sincerely,

Frank Freidel (LVG)

Frank Freidel
Charles Warren Professor of
American History

FF:LVG

Dictated but not read.

WILLIAM CLYDE FRIDAY *(in 1963) president of the University of North Carolina system*

I remembered his (Kennedy's) visit to Chapel Hill on a beautiful October day in 1962, when 35,000 people in Kenan Stadium heard him speak after the University of North Carolina conferred upon him an honorary doctor's degree (the first such degree conferred upon him, I think, after his assumption of office). James Reston of The New York Times *said to me later, "When we left Washington, the President had lines in his face, and his shoulders stooped. But after he had stood there before 35,000 cheering people, and after he had gone to Fort Bragg and seen a demonstration of America's enormous military firepower, the lines vanished from his face and he began to stand erect again. One could see that it served the President well to leave the Capitol and visit the people.*

CATHY FUNK *(in 1963) seven-year-old resident of Tennessee*

I was with my parents and sister traveling and at the time we heard the news on the car radio, we were between Kansas City and St. Louis. My dad pulled over to a roadside park where many other cars (approximately 30–40) had stopped. These strangers clustered together in several groups and discussed the news for 30–40 minutes. I was too young to be aware of the seriousness of this event, but I will always remember how all these people seemed to suddenly have "so much to talk about," and were sharing their thoughts and emotions with complete strangers.

INDIRA GANDHI, *Prime Minister of India*

3231

12, Willingdon Crescent
New Delhi 110 011
India

October 12, 1979

Dear Mrs Hansen,

I have received your letter of September, the 4th.

There was a general feeling of shock at the news of
the assassination of President Kennedy. He had captured
the imagination of people in India as in other countries,
and his image was one of a person who could give new
direction and dynamism to American public life. We were
amazed that the vast networks of intelligence and security
which surround the President of America were incapable of
forewarning him and preventing the tragedy. I was in Delhi
when the news came. I do not remember exactly what I was
doing, but my father and I felt deeply grieved, especially
as we had visited with and got to know President Kennedy.
Jacqueline Kennedy had stayed in our home as our personal
guest. We deeply abhor the politics of violence.

Good wishes for your project.

Yours sincerely,

Indira Gandhi

Indira Gandhi

Mrs Jodie Elliot Hansen
Union City
U S A

JACK GERTZ *(in 1963) AT&T representative with the White House press corps, in Dallas on November 22*

It was perhaps the most dramatic and one of the saddest days of my life. I was riding in the White House press bus in the Dallas motorcade, sitting in one of the front seats next to Tom Wicker, White House correspondent for The New York Times. *I remember that many people on the parade route were carrying or holding signs—some pro-Kennedy and some anti-Kennedy. There was one particular sign I will never forget. It read: "Please, Mr. Kennedy, give us another ex-President." It was about the length of a bus, held by about 15 people and I feel sure this was one of the last ones the President saw. We all shook our heads in disbelief when seeing it.*

I did not hear the shots fired. We were not aware of any trouble until we saw a policeman on a motorcycle as he jumped off, drew his pistol, and began running. Looking ahead, we saw the presidential limousine taking off, full-speed ahead. Sitting high on the bus, we had an unobstructed view of the vehicles ahead but were still unaware of the nature of the obvious trouble. Looking to the right, we observed people falling to the ground. Some of them were running and one young couple pushed their child to the ground, covering him with their bodies for protection.

The policemen who were handling the motorcade signaled to our driver to follow them and escorted us to the Mart. The people there were quite upset.

(continued)

Some were crying and asking, "Is it true? Did they shoot the President? Is he dead?" We immediately contacted Robert Manning, the White House transportation officer, who told us to go to Parkland and be prepared to assist in providing telephone service for this emergency situation.

Everyone wanted a telephone. Everyone needed a telephone. Everyone was begging for a telephone. There had not been enough time to set up a teletype system and it goes without saying that there were not nearly enough telephones at the hospital before the additional ones were installed.

There was still no official report on the President's condition. When the word came that the President was dead, we knew additional facilities would have to be set up at Love Field. Again the Southwestern Bell people responded in a prompt and efficient manner. Vice President Johnson was hurriedly and secretly rushed to Air Force One at Love Field and his swearing-in as our new President took place in the cabin of the plane. President Kennedy's body was also carried to Air Force One for the return trip to Washington. It goes without saying, the return trip to Washington was under changed conditions. It was virtually impossible to relax. All of us felt an emotional drain beyond comprehension. The atmosphere on the plane was unreal. Some of us were quite emotional and a few of the women cried continuously. There were bloodshot eyes all around. Many of us had known and had traveled with JFK for years. We had a very special feeling for him and the sadness was overwhelming.

JOHN GLENN, *U.S. Senator from Arizona, former astronaut*

United States Senate

COMMITTEE ON
GOVERNMENTAL AFFAIRS
WASHINGTON, DC 20510

November 18, 1985

Mrs. Jodie Elliott Hansen
Box 1031
Union City, Tennessee   38261

Dear Mrs Hansen:

Thank you for your inquiry about my reaction to the assassination of John F. Kennedy.

I was still in the Mercury Space Program then, and I heard the news on my car radio as I drove through Dallas. I was deeply shocked and saddened, and when I learned that America had lost a President, I knew that I had also lost a friend. After November 22, 1963 I felt that America had lost her innocence, and that in some ways we would never be quite so young again.

Best regards.

Sincerely,

John Glenn
United States Senator

JG/ca

HARRY GOLDEN, *publisher*, The Carolina Israelite

THE CAROLINA ISRAELITE
THE MOST WIDELY QUOTED PERSONAL JOURNAL IN THE WORLD
HARRY GOLDEN. EDITOR

BOOKS BY HARRY GOLDEN

ONLY IN AMERICA
FOR 2¢ PLAIN
ENJOY, ENJOY
CARL SANDBURG
YOU'RE ENTITLE
FORGOTTEN PIONEER
MR. KENNEDY AND THE NEGROES
SO WHAT ELSE IS NEW?
THE SPIRIT OF THE GHETTO
A LITTLE GIRL IS DEAD
ESS, ESS, MEIN KINDT
(EAT, EAT, MY CHILD)
THE BEST OF HARRY GOLDEN
THE RIGHT TIME (THE AUTOBIOGRAPHY
OF HARRY GOLDEN)
SO LONG AS YOU'RE HEALTHY
THE ISRAELIS
GOLDEN BOOK OF JEWISH HUMOR
THE GREATEST JEWISH CITY
IN THE WORLD
TRAVELS THROUGH JEWISH AMERICA
OUR SOUTHERN LANDSMAN
LONG LIVE COLUMBUS
—AMERICA I LOVE YOU!

November 12, 1978

Dear Mrs. ~~Habon~~ Hannon!:

On that sad day, the Norman Luboff Choir had
a scheduled concert at the Ovens Auditorium in
Charlotte, Whihch of course was cabcekked.
Later that evening Mr. Luboff and his choir came
to my house and I delivered a short lecture on the
assassination. I told them that the Irish very ~~santhmush~~
seriously say that they are descended from Irish
kings. The old legends tell of tall men, full of
grace and dignit y, brave, wise, generiusly giving
of themselves for the good of all. These were the
kings of Ireland.
They seemed only legends until we were given
one of their sons for too brief a time. Now we know
the legends are true. We can send down words
telling of noble deeds that will become legendsin
their tun of a great and beloved leader, John
Fitzgerald Kennedy, wothy son of kingly forebear.

PLEASE REPLY TO 1701 E. 8TH STREET, CHARLOTTE, NORTH CAROLINA 28204 / TELEPHONE 376-3388 — 376-5814

THE CAROLINA ISRAELITE

THE MOST WIDELY QUOTED PERSONAL JOURNAL IN THE WORLD
HARRY GOLDEN, EDITOR

BOOKS BY HARRY GOLDEN

ONLY IN AMERICA
FOR 2¢ PLAIN
ENJOY, ENJOY
CARL SANDBURG
YOU'RE ENTITLE
FORGOTTEN PIONEER
MR. KENNEDY AND THE NEGROES
SO WHAT ELSE IS NEW?
THE SPIRIT OF THE GHETTO
A LITTLE GIRL IS DEAD
ESS, ESS, MEIN KINDT
  (EAT, EAT, MY CHILD)
THE BEST OF HARRY GOLDEN
THE RIGHT TIME (THE AUTOBIOGRAPHY
  OF HARRY GOLDEN)
SO LONG AS YOU'RE HEALTHY
THE ISRAELIS
GOLDEN BOOK OF JEWISH HUMOR
THE GREATEST JEWISH CITY
  IN THE WORLD
TRAVELS THROUGH JEWISH AMERICA
OUR SOUTHERN LANDSMAN
LONG LIVE COLUMBUS
  —AMERICA I LOVE YOU!

Then th Norman Luboff choir sang "WE SHALL
OVERCOME-SOMEDAY."

Harry Golden

Harry Golden

*Please excuse the typing. My
secretary is home sick.*

PLEASE REPLY TO 1701 E. 8TH STREET, CHARLOTTE, NORTH CAROLINA 28204 / TELEPHONE 376-3388 — 376-5814

BARRY GOLDWATER
ARIZONA

United States Senate

WASHINGTON, D.C. 20510

COMMITTEES:

ARMED SERVICES
  TACTICAL AIR POWER SUBCOMMITTEE
  INTELLIGENCE SUBCOMMITTEE
  RESEARCH AND DEVELOPMENT SUBCOMMITTEE
COMMERCE, SCIENCE AND TRANSPORTATION
  SCIENCE, TECHNOLOGY AND SPACE
  AVIATION
  COMMUNICATIONS
SELECT COMMITTEE ON INTELLIGENCE
  VICE CHAIRMAN

September 4, 1979

Mrs. Jodie Elliott Hansen
Box 1031
Union City, Tennessee 38261

Dear Mrs. Hansen:

On November the 22nd, 1963, my wife and I were flying from
Phoenix, Arizona, to Muncie, Indiana, escorting the body
of her mother who had passed away in her home in Phoenix.
Muncie was her hometown so we were taking her body there
for burial.

When I got off the airplane in Chicago, we were met by our
nephew to be escorted to a private airplane which we flew
to Muncie; and it was he who told me about the assassination.

Sincerely,

Barry Goldwater

W. WILSON GOODE, *first African American mayor of Philadelphia*

CITY OF PHILADELPHIA

W. WILSON GOODE
MAYOR

February 6, 1984

Mrs. Jodie Elliott Hansen
Box 1031
Union City, Tennessee   38261

Dear Mrs. Hansen:

I am responding to your request of January 22nd concerning my memories of the day John F. Kennedy was assassinated.

On November 22, 1963, I was working in private industry in the area of West Philadelphia. I had gone to a small luncheonette nearby my office, and I had just received my order when the news of the President's being shot came over the radio. I simply got up and paid my bill with no further thought of eating that day.

The sense of shock and deep sadness did not leave me for some days afterward and was only abated somewhat when I was able to share my deep feelings with my family.

I hope the foregoing will be helpful to you in the preparation of your book.

Sincerely,

W. WILSON GOODE

WWG:edf

BENNY GOODMAN, *jazz and swing musician and bandleader*

BENNY GOODMAN
200 EAST 66TH STREET
NEW YORK, N. Y. 10021
—
TEMPLETON 8-5280

22 July 1985

Mrs. Jodie Elliott Hansen
Box 1031
Union City, TN 38261

Dear Mrs. Hansen,

Your book on individual reactions to Kennedy's assassination
sounds very interesting. It is indeed a moment that stands
out in the memory. I was sitting with members of my band
eating lunch in a restaurant, somewhere in the Texas
Panhandle. The news about Kennedy came on a television in
an adjacent room. We seemed to be the only ones to even notice.

Good luck with your book,

Sincerely,

Benny Goodman

A. J. Goodpaster, *U.S. Army General, Superintendent, U.S. Military Academy*

OFFICE OF THE SUPERINTENDENT
UNITED STATES MILITARY ACADEMY
WEST POINT, NEW YORK 10996

MAIO

21 June 1979

Dear Mrs. Hansen:

Many thanks for your May 17 letter requesting information about both my personal and West Point's reaction to the assassination of President Kennedy.

Though I was not at West Point during this time frame, members of my staff who were here advise me that West Point's general reaction was pretty much the same as it was elsewhere; shock and disbelief. Adding somewhat to the confusion, initial news reports were not clear regarding the grave condition of the President. Subsequent news of Mr. Kennedy's death changed the mood to what could best be described as deep grief. The inclosed copies from the November 29, 1963 issue of the post newspaper, POINTER VIEW, do a fine job of summarizing campus reaction to the assassination and follow-on ceremonies held in honor of the slain President.

On the personal side, I was then Assistant to the Chairman of the Joint Chiefs of Staff, and was preparing to attend a meeting with a German delegation headed by General Foertsch, the head of their armed forces.

During or just after the lunch hour, before the meeting started, we heard an initial report that the President had been shot, that the injury was serious, but that his condition was not known. As I recall, General Maxwell Taylor, the Chairman of the Joint Chiefs of Staff and a close friend of the President, received a call from the President's brother, Robert, just before we went into the meeting.

While the meeting was in session, word was brought in that the President had died. General Taylor announced this to the group; there was a moment of silence, followed by expressions of sympathy and condolence from the German visitors, and the meeting was brought to a close.

(continued)

MAIO   21 June 1979

Within the Joint Chiefs of Staff organization, we made an immediate
check to determine whether the Vice President was safe, and whether
there had been attacks against any other high figures in the government.
Also, we quickly transmitted information to commands all around the
world of the events that had occurred.

I hope this information proves helpful in development of your project.

With best wishes from West Point,

                              Sincerely,

1 Incl
As stated   A. J. GOODPASTER
                              Lt. General, U.S. Army
                              Superintendent

Mrs. Jodie Elliott Hansen
Box 1031
Union City, Tennessee 38261

FREDDY GREEN *(in 1963) death row prisoner at the Tennessee State Penitentiary*

Unlike the people in the free world, or the prisoners in the main populations, we were not allowed radios or televisions. Our only mode of communication was via mail. As a result, when the news of John F. Kennedy's assassination reached Death Row, he had been dead some nine hours. At the time of this tragic news I was in the process of writing my lawyer, seeking an appeal to the United States Supreme Court. Hearing that the President was dead, I put aside this important communications to my lawyer. There were two men scheduled to die in the electric chair about this time. These men, surprisingly, set aside their efforts to get stays of execution, to solemnly express their hurt over this tragedy.

JOHNNY GREEN, *Oscar-winning composer and songwriter*

JOHN GREEN

903 NORTH BEDFORD DRIVE   BEVERLY HILLS, CALIFORNIA 90210   213-271-5504   213-276-3061

November 2, 1983

Mrs. Jodie Elliott Hansen
Box 1031
Union City, TN 38261

IN RE:-J.F. KENNEDY ASSASSINATION
YOURS OF OCTOBER 27, 1983

Dear Jodie Hansen:-

I was on the telephone, on a long distance call to New York City, when the gentleman to whom I was speaking, whose office radio was on in the background, suddenly exclaimed, "Oh! My God! Hold on a minute!" In a matter of seconds he was back on the line telling me, in a voice charged with frantic emotion, "The President has just been shot in Dallas!" I instantly said, "I'll get back to you later; I'm going to turn the news on. Good-bye." ---I turned on the TV and already the News Department had taken over, and was reporting those ghastly minutes immediately following the shooting. Like everyone else, I remained glued to the TV from that moment on, too stunned to weep, as shocked and saddened as one could possibly be.

The following Sunday afternoon, as part of the national round-robin of the nation's leading Symphony Orchestras, I, as a then Associate Conductor of the Los Angeles Philharmonic Orchestra, tearfully conducted the Orchestra in Samuel Barber's "ADAGIO FOR STRINGS" as part of a Memorial Concert for President Kennedy at The Los Angeles Sports Arena. The remainder of The Los Angeles Philharmonic's portion of the National Tribute by the major Symphony Orchestras was conducted by The Orchestra's Music Director, Zubin Mehta. It was THE DIES IRAE from the VERDI REQUIEM with Mary Costa as Soloist.

My thanks to you for including me among those whose comments you have sought.

Sincerely yours,

JOHN (JOHNNY) GREEN

JG:dn

114

LYNN GREENWALT, *Director, U.S. Fish and Wildlife Service*

Full Name Lynn A. Greenwalt   *Age* 48

Current Address Rockville, Md.   *Address Nov. '63* Albuquerque, N. Mex.

Occupation or Profession now Director, U.S. Fish and Wildlife Service, Dept. of the Interior
Occupation or Profession Nov. '63 Planner, U.S. Fish and Wildlife Service

Use space below and please include small details such as: if you saved any newspaper clippings or memorial publications; if you had ever seen or met President Kennedy; if you (at the time) were worried or apprehensive about the possibility of a world crisis or a conspiracy; if your community had special memorial or any special church services, etc.

At the time of the assasination I was working in the Regional Office of the U.S. Fish and Wildlife Service in Albuquerque, New Mexico. The office was a large one, with perhaps 175 employees on several floors of a Federal office building in that city.

I can recall that shortly after the assassination --though we did not know what it was at the time, of course-- there was a generall buzz of excitement and uncertainty in the building. I can recall vividly that the telephones in my office, where there were several lines and therfore several of the lighted line access buttons for each telephone, were all lighted as outsiders tried to call in or those employees in the office tried to call out to learn what was happening.

By sheerest good fortune my wife, who lived several miles away from the office, had been able to get an open line and call me to inform me of the happenings in Dallas. For some time I was one of the few people in my office who possessed anything like current information on the affair. However, as others heard from wives and others who heard radio or TV news began to amplify the news, we were able to follow events as they unfolded.

I recall that the news was greated with a solemn hush; no sense of urgency or of panic or concern, just a sort of subdued buzz as folks shared information about the tragedy. There was no sense of concern about possible actions like general terrorism perpetrated by the assassins, or of attempts on the lives of other public figures. There were conflicting stories about what had happened to the President --the details, anyway-- and the complex array of sub-stories about who had seen what and the like. There was a good deal of confusion about the details, but no uncertainty about the fact that the President had been shot.

I remember that some of the employees in the office --many of whom were

(continued)

of Spanish-American heritage, left the office to go to a nearby Catholic Church to pray, but returned later in the day to continue their work.

In recalling those events, I am struck by the fact that at no time was there any discussion of the possibility of this event leading to serious political or governmental repercussions. None of us gave any thought to the possibility that there might be a danger to the continuation of the orderly business of government or that this might be a prelude to some attempt totally to disrupt the government. In retrospect, I feel this is because we had yet to see the effects of terrorism as later practiced in other parts of the world; we had solid confidence in the continuation of government and we all knew that a President --the man-- might be destroyed, but that the Presidency --the institution-- would continue.

I remember that by far the most dramatic impact upon my own family (my wife and two very young boys) came when Jack Ruby killed Oswald in front of TV cameras and thereby drove home to millions of viewers the violence of the overall affair.

My own feeling is that the Kennedy assassination could be characterized as the last of of its kind: one filled with horror and disbelief and a deep sadness, as was the case with Lincoln and the others. It did not have the immediate poltical and conspiratorial overtones --or the massive revolting reaction that subsequent acts of violence have had. Perhaps this is because until that time there has been little in the way of organized political violence associated with these acts, in this country or elsewhere. We had always expected that these kinds of things could be done by twisted person-alities, driven by their own demons or perceptions of wrongdoings against them. We had not come to learn about the ruthless, organized, highly political killings and acts of terror that have been so common in the last decade. We we shocked, striken, and deeply sorry, but had not yet learned that there are people capable of using terror and assassination as a means to an organized political end. We were innocent in ways we no longer are.

Lynn A. Greenwalt

GERMAINE GREER, *author, feminist activist*

Tulsa Center for the Study of Women's Literature
Germaine Greer, Director

7 October 1981

Mrs. Jodie Elliott Hansen
Box 1031
Union City, Tennessee
38261

Dear Mrs. Jodie Elliott Hansen,

On the day President Kennedy was assassinated, I was woken by a friend beating on the door of my tiny garden flat in Sydney. I remember sitting on the door-step in the bright sunlight and staring at the river pebbles in the garden for a very long time. On that day I stopped being afraid of spiders, men loitering by dark corners and the black and yellow hordes. I began to be afraid of Amerika.

Yours faithfully,

Germaine Greer

The University of Tulsa   600 South College Ave.   Tulsa, Oklahoma 74104   (918) 592-6000 ext. 503

W. EDWARD GRIFFIS *(in 1963) pharmaceutical sales rep in Jackson, Tennessee*

I left for home in Memphis, following the events on my car radio. The expressway was not complete then, so I had to drive through several small towns. One of my most vivid memories was seeing the people in these small towns gathered in clusters in deep conversation, and on the downtown streets people were also in small groups. Had I not known what had happened, I would've been very puzzled because the sight was most unusual.

ROBERT GURALNIK *(in 1963) professional pianist*

I was in Amsterdam and vividly remember what an emotional impact the death of President Kennedy had on the people there. People on the streets were wearing black armbands as a sign of mourning. They seemed to feel as though they had lost their best friend. All the people of Europe were captivated with Kennedy in an extraordinary way.

ALEXANDER M. HAIG, JR., *U.S. Secretary of State*

Washington Office: 1155 15th Street, N.W. Suite 800 Washington, D.C. 20005 (202) 429-9788 - 429-0039

February 18, 1983

Dear Mrs. Hansen:

Thank you for your recent letter and for the opportunity to relate what I recall was my preoccupation at the time of hearing of the assassination of President John F. Kennedy.

On that fateful day in 1963, I was at my desk in the Pentagon and, as my duties required as Military Assistant to the Secretary of the Army, Cyrus Vance, I immediately became involved in planning and coordinating for the funeral of the deceased President. The day and hour on hearing the report will remain as today as one of shock and suspicion regarding the events leading to his untimely death.

Again, I appreciate the opportunity to contribute to your efforts and extend to you my best wishes although it would be my pleasure rather to respond to events which recall pleasant memories of my public service. Your efforts to document personal accounts is, of course, understood and respected.

Sincerely,

Alexander M. Haig, Jr.

Mrs. Jodie Elliott Hansen
Box 1031
Union City, Tennessee 98261

Home Office: Quaker Ridge Road, Croton-on-Hudson, NY 10520 (914) 762-0700

Received May 18, 1979

Mrs Jodie Elliott Hansen
Box 1031
Union City, Tennessee 38

l Name William Hanchett   Age 56

rent Address San Diego, California   Address Nov. '63 same

upation or Profession now Professor of History

upation or Profession Nov. '63 same

space below and please include small details, such as: if you saved an
spaper clippings or memorial publications; if you had ever seen or met
sident Kennedy; if you (at the time) were worried or apprehensive abou
possibility of a world crisis or a conspiracy; if your community had
cial church or memorial services, etc. Any small detail is important.

In November 1963 I was browsing in the bookstore on the university campus
where I teach. As soon as I went outside I could tell something was wrong;
there was no activity. Instead of hurrying along to or from classes, the students were gathered in small groups listening to portable radios. When I learn
what had happened, my automatic reaction was to re-enter the bookstore where
nobody had heard the ghastly news and life was proceeding normally. It was as
if I thought I could turn back time and continue to live in a world in which
the assassination had not taken place.

You asked me to comment upon how the news of Lincoln's death was spread.
It was by telegraph, of course, to the newspapers throughout the North. Some
New York morning papers even carried the announcement on April 15. Military
commanders were informed promptly by telegraph also, though the news was usuall
withheld from U. S. troops in the South for several days, for fear violent
retaliation would be taken against southerners. Many ardent supporters of the
Confederacy hated Lincoln with a passion it is difficult for us to appreciate,
and some of them reacted as Booth had expected most of them would—enthusiastic
But most southerners, the ones who recognized that the South was defeated beyond
any possibility of revival, soon recognized that with Lincoln's death they had
lost a compassionate enemy, that the assassin's bullet could only make things
harder for them. So, if they did not mourn Lincoln, they at least regretted
Booth.

Good luck with your very interesting project.

William Hanchett

HAL HARDIN *(in 1963) Peace Corps volunteer living in a South American jungle*

On November 22, 1963, I was walking up a gangplank when an acquaintance of mine told me about President Kennedy. My friend was a white mercenary soldier who had recently returned from fighting in the Congo. Being a mercenary and accustomed to death and violence, he was very matter of fact about the incident. I think that he was happy that the President had been killed. My reaction was numbness and anger. I had joined the Peace Corps because of the President and I felt that a bit of me had died in Dallas and at that time I started to doubt whether any of our work (or anything else) was worthwhile....On the boat there were some American and European oil men, and they were elated that the President was dead. Before the boat sailed I walked into Cartagena and the people there were crying and in a state of shock. The Colombians loved Kennedy.

MILLIE HARRISON *(in 1963) telephone switchboard operator in*
Union City, Tennessee

An unidentified lady dialed "Operator" and told me that while she was watching her program, As the World Turns, *there was a news bulletin saying the President had just been shot. Within 2–3 seconds the whole switchboard lit up like I had never seen, with people making long-distance calls. In fact, there were so many calls coming in that within a few minutes we had a power failure and went on the emergency generator for 2–3 minutes. People who were making local calls had to wait several seconds and sometimes minutes before hearing a dial tone.*

ORRIN G. HATCH, *U.S. Senator from Utah*

ORRIN G. HATCH
UTAH

125 RUSSELL SENATE OFFICE BUILDING
TELEPHONE: (202) 224-5251

HATCH HOT LINE 1-800-662-4300
(UTAH TOLL FREE)

𝔘nited 𝔖tates 𝔖enate
WASHINGTON, D.C. 20510

COMMITTEES:
JUDICIARY
LABOR AND HUMAN
RESOURCES
SMALL BUSINESS
BUDGET
OFFICE OF TECHNOLOGY
ASSESSMENT

September 1, 1981

Mrs. Jodie Elliott Hansen
Post Office Box 1031
Union City, Tennessee   38261

Dear Mrs. Hansen:

You may use the following paragraph in your book:

At the time of the news of the
assassination of President John Kennedy,
I was an attorney in Pittsburgh, Pennsylvania. I had just gone to the county
morgue with regard to the case I had
been working on. I can remember what a
chilling effect the assassination had
upon me. I immediately offered a prayer
in my heart for the family of President
Kennedy and spent the rest of the day
chatting with family and friends about
the terrible news.

I hope this helps you.

Warmest regards,

Orrin G. Hatch
United States Senator

OGH:hl

EDITH HEAD, *Oscar-winning costume designer*

MCΛ

NIVERSAL CITY STUDIOS, INC., 100 UNIVERSAL CITY PLAZA, UNIVERSAL CITY, CA. 91608, 213-985-4321

March 14, 1980

Mrs. Jodie Elliott Hansen
Box 1031
Union City, Tennessee 38261

Dear Mrs. Hansen:

In answer to the questions you ask in
your letter, I do not remember what I was doing when I
heard that President Kennedy had been assassinated, but
my feelings were the same as they would be for any human
being who had been shot.

Cordially,

Edith Head

EH:sj

123

GEORGETOWN UNIVERSITY

WASHINGTON, D. C. 20057

OFFICE OF THE PRESIDENT

October 28, 1981

Mrs. Jodie Elliott Hansen
Box 131
Union City, Tennessee 38261

Dear Mrs. Hansen:

Sometimes times make a big difference, and for me the assassination of President Kennedy occurred at night. I was studying at Oxford, and having a dinner at a restaurant with a fellow graduate student. We were both Americans, and at the very end of our dinner, about 9:00 p.m., a gentleman leaned across from a near-by table and said, "Forgive me for interrupting, but I could tell you were American, and I judged from your conversation that you did not know the President was shot this afternoon". He did not know whether or not he had been hit or hit badly, and since the head waiter was a friend, I called him over. He told me that his wife had telephoned him and that the President had been hit and was in a hospital. My fellow student and I paid the bill quickly, rushed back to our college, and downstairs to a T.V. room. Obviously everyone in the room had heard the full news, since when the two of us came in (we were the only Yanks in college that night) they stood up, made a place for us in front of the T.V. set. The opening announcement of the BBC 9:00 news was the simple rather terrible statement, "President Kennedy is dead". There were then the T.V. pictures of the actual shooting, and a few comments and analyses. The whole news program was obviously muted, and when it was over, the BBC closed it by running a picture of the American flag and playing the Star Spangled Banner. It wasn't until 11:00 p.m. that night we found out who the assailant was, and of course the next morning the full details were in the <u>Times</u> and the <u>Guardian</u>.

The assassination began for us an extraordinary week. It was impossible in Oxford to move around without perfect strangers coming up to tell you how sorry they were. If you took clothes in to be cleaned, or stopped to buy a pack of cigarettes, as soon as the American accent was recognized, whoever it was, would tell you with absolute and complete sincerity, sometimes with tears, how bad they felt about what

had happened, and how sorry they were. The continental press
began probing immediately for plots and interesting political
conclusions. The English press with enormous dignity dealt
with sorrow. The English people did the same. I had never
realized as fully how much our common language made us
understand one another. What the English understood about
Americans was that so large a part of our reaction was shame.
Hence the dignity and the restraint of the coverage.

Most people don't know it, but the horrendous picture of
the murder of Oswald was run only once on BBC T.V. Everyone
in England felt that it was too brutal and ridiculous an
anti-climax, and both press and T.V. by and large covered it,
but not sensationally.

Towards the end of the next week the University and the
town decided that a memorial ceremony would be appropriate,
and the principal one held in Oxford was held in a tiny Roman
Catholic parish on the very edge of the town. To it on a
Friday evening came the entire University brass in cap and
gown, as well as literally hundreds of dons and students, also
in formal academic attire. On the other side came the entire
civic corporation, headed by the Lord Mayor, in full civic
regalia. Three American priests said the Mass, and a fourth
American preached at it.

I wonder if I am at all exceptional among your
respondents in telling you how intensly painful it is to
remember those moments.

Yours sincerely,

Timothy S. Healy, S.J.

TSH:ljb

W. R. Hearst, Jr., *publisher, Hearst Newspapers,*
Pulitzer Prize–winning journalist

HEARST NEWSPAPERS

959 EIGHTH AVE.   NEW YORK, N.Y. 10019

OFFICE OF THE
EDITOR-IN-CHIEF

March 18, 1981

(212) 262-8898

Mrs. Jodie Elliott Hansen
Box 1031
Union City, TN 38261

Dear Mrs. Hansen:

As both my wife and I were very close personal
friends of Jack Kennedy (he had been a mild beau of
hers in the middle '40s) plus the fact that Jack was
killed on her birthday) the horrible incident is
indelibly impressed on our minds.

Austine and I were sunning ourselves on the
beach outside a hotel in North Miami Beach. I think
it was the Normandy. Jack had addressed a meeting of
the Inter American Press Association there the night
before, as I recall.

Somebody (maybe it was me) had a radio which
was tuned to the President's arrival and was covering
his fatal trip in the car. The incredibility of what
the announcer was saying just froze all of us in the
position that we were in when he first told of hearing
the shot and telling graphically of the fact that the
President was slumped over, etc. I don't think any-
body moved for five minutes. The news was too horrifying
and shocking for anyone to really believe.

I think I've answered your four points, though
possibly not in the order in which you listed them.

Sincerely,

W. R. Hearst, Jr.

je

126

DR. HENRY J. HEIMLICH, *physician, inventor of the "Heimlich maneuver"*

I was sitting in the auditorium of Memorial Hospital in New York City attending a meeting of the New York Society of Thoracic Surgeons, an organization of chest surgeons. A prominent British thoracic surgeon had come from London as the guest speaker. He was about to be introduced when one of the doctors came into the room, walked to the podium and announced "President Kennedy has been shot." He had heard the report on the radio and there were no other facts available. The speaker started his lecture when, a few minutes later, the doctor who had made the announcement returned and said President Kennedy had died.

We all sat silently. My sympathies were as much for the speaker, at that time, as for President Kennedy. He obviously felt obligated to continue his presentation and talked on hesitatingly as the audience silently looked on expressionless. After three or four minutes, the only black surgeon in the society suddenly stood up and walked out the rear door. It appeared to be symbolic that he was the first person so moved.

I was torn between the tragedy of the moment and courtesy to the surgeon who had come from so far to deliver his lecture. I lasted only a few minutes longer and then was compelled to walk up the aisle and out the rear door.

I got to my car and listened to reports while driving the long hour to our house in Rye, New York. Like everyone else in the country, on arriving home, I stayed glued to the television set.

6/3/83

Henry J. Heimlich, M.D.

HJH/cjp

REV. THEODORE M. HESBURGH, *president, University of Notre Dame*

Full name Rev. Theodore M. HESBURGH, C.S.C.   Age 61
Current address Univ. of Notre Dame, IN.   Address Nov. '63 Same
Occupation or Profession now Priest - President N.D.
Occupation or Profession Nov. '63 same
Use space below and please include small details, such as: if you saved a
newspaper clippings or memorial publications; if you had ever seen or met
President Kennedy; if you (at the time) were worried or apprehensive about
the possibility of a world crisis or a conspiracy; if your community had
special church or memorial services, etc. Any small detail is important.

At the time President Kennedy was shot, I was inspecting, with other members of
the National Science Board, the site for an atmospheric research center at
Boulder, Colorado. We came down the mountain to have lunch with President
Joseph Smiley of the University of Colorado at his home. On entering the
drive way, we heard of the shoting of the President. Our first reaction was
one of incredulity. Then we huddled around the radio in the kitchen until
the report of his death came through. It was a very somber lunch.

After lunch, there was an effort to continue the meeting of the National Science
Board, but it only lasted about five minutes. I then left and returned to the
University on the first available plane, arriving in Chicago around midnight
and spending the night at the Notre Dame High School there. Upon arriving at
the high school, I called Father Edmund P. Joyce, our Executive Vice President,
who was with our team in Iowa where we were to play the University of Iowa
in football the next day. He told me that the University of Iowa wished to
continue the game with some kind of a ceremony at half time, but I told him
it was best that we cancel the game, which we did, promising a rebate on
tickets that had been bought. Personally, I did not think there would be
many requests for rebates, but, in fact, there were over $90,000.00 worth.
This came as a great surprise, but, in any case, we paid off, as we had
promised.

Many other teams went ahead and played their games, but I think it was a
mistake. In any event, I'm glad we didn't. I remember saying that if the
President's tragic death was not reason for calling off a football game,
then I could not imagine what would be.

I was not on campus at the time, but I was told that the universal reaction

there was to come to Church to pray and that there were immediately
organized Requiem Masses for the President. When I did return to
the University, I was asked by the Kennedys to come to Washington
for the funeral. I did attend the funeral as one of the few priests
in the sanctuary with Cardinal Cushing and the Apostolic Delegate.
The other priest was John Kennedy's cousin, Father Fitzgerald.
It was a sad day.

AL HIRSCHFELD, *caricaturist*

AL HIRSCHFELD
122 EAST 95th STREET
NEW YORK, N. Y. 10028
—
   TEL. 534-6172

        JODIE ELLIOTT HANSEN
        Box # 1031
        Union City, Tennessee 38261

   Dear Ms. HANSEN:

             On that unforgettable day I was
   serving as a juror in the Supreme Court, New
   York City. I forget what the case was all about
   but I remember with bitter clarity the bailiff
   whispering to the Judge, the frightened look
   of unbelievability etched on his face, and the
   tremulouss announcement to the jurors ,witnesses
   and guests that our President had been assassinated
   and the Court would be closed as of that moment
   until further notice.

                        Sincerely,

                        HIRSCHFELD   N.Y. TIMES

             November 30th 1982

AL HIRT, *trumpeter and bandleader, played at President Kennedy's inauguration*

January 17, 1980

Mrs. Jodie Elliott Hansen
Box 1031
Union City, Tennessee 38261

Dear Mrs. Hansen:

I was at home watching TV when I heard the shocking
news. I was stunned and not really knowing how to
express my feelings, I continued watching and saw another
one of my heros, Walter Conkite, cry. I drove down to
my club on Bourbon Street which at that time of the day
was empty and desolate with remains from the previous
night's revelry. I locked myself in, picked up my horn
and played the blues. Being all alone and blowing blues
seemed to allow me some release for the strong emotion
I felt.

After a time, I secured a black wreath, put it on my
night club door and remained closed for business until
after his funeral.

Sincerely,

Al Hirt

AH:ps

(504) 525-6167
809 ST. LOUIS STREET
NEW ORLEANS, LOUISIANA 70112

MILES H. HODGES *(in 1963) graduate student at Georgetown University*

I remember that evening seeing Johnson deplane and speak his first words as President —thinking of the great loss of style that was occurring within the White House. I did not fret for the Union. I really did not think strategically but rather personally. My president was dead. I naturally attended the funeral procession a few days later. The shock was over—but not the sense of loss. Shortly after that I was interviewing the Ethiopian ambassador on other matters, but found that the ambassador kept coming back to Kennedy. He wanted to share with me his sense of personal loss. I remember being impressed with the fact that other people of other countries related in this same personal way—a way I was never able to muster in my feelings about Johnson.

HAL HOLBROOK, *Emmy- and Tony-winning actor*

Hal Holbrook

Dec. 3, 1979

Mrs. Jodie Elliott Hansen
Box 1031
Union City, Tenn. 38261

Dear Mrs. Hansen:

I was rehearsing for Arthur Miller's play,
After The Fall, down on Second Avenue in
New York City. I had walked across town
from my apartment that morning, unaware of
anything unusual happening, and when I got
in the elevator to go up to the rehearsal
floor the operator mumbled something like,
"What do you think about the President?"
I half understood him and said, "What about
the President...?" at which point the elevator
doors opened and I saw Jason Robards standing
in the hall looking directly at me. His face
was so drawn and the look on his face so distraught that I knew without asking that something terrible had happened to Kennedy. Then
they told me that he had been shot.

No one was able to work. The rehearsal was
cancelled and everyone left.

Good luck with your book.

Yours,

Hal Holbrook

BOB HOPE

February 19, 1981

Mrs. Jodie Elliott Hansen
Box 1031
Union City, Tennessee 38261

Dear Mrs. Hansen:

In answer to your letter about what I was
doing, my reaction and the reaction of others
at the time of the assination of President
John F. Kennedy:

I was playing golf at the Oakmont Country Club
in Glendale (California) when the caddy master
ran out to us and told us that President Kennedy
was assinated. Of course we, like the rest of
the world, were very shocked. We ran into the
golf shop and watched the television news and
I guess experienced the same kind of sadness
that everybody else did.

Earlier in 1963 I had a couple of meetings with
President Kennedy. I got to know him quite well
and he had a fine sense of humor and was doing
a great job for our country.

A very tragic moment, for not only myself, but
the entire world.

Regards,

BOB HOPE

BH:mg

FIGHT BACK! WITH DAVID HOROWITZ®

1982 EMMY WINNERS
Public Affairs Program
Program Host

©ATAS/NATAS

June 29, 1982

Mrs. Jodie Elliott Hansen
Box 1031
Union City, Tennessee 38261

Dear Jodie:

I am most interested in your work, and I have enclosed my comments and recollections on the Assassination of President John F. Kennedy.

I would appreciate it if, when your work is published, you could send me a copy of it.

Best of luck on the project.

Cheerfully,

David Horowitz

3000 West Alameda Avenue, Burbank, California 91523 (213) 840-4444

Distributed By
CONTEMPO TV LTD.

DAVID HOROWITZ, CONSUMER ADVOCATE - Recollections on the Assassination of President John F. Kennedy:

When John F. Kennedy was assassinated, I was working as an editor at NBC News in New York and I received one of the first bulletins that said: "Shots rang out in Dallas and President Kennedy was apparently wounded." I was so shocked by the wire copy that I sat and looked at it for several seconds, that seemed like hours. I then quickly ran through the NBC newsroom informing the producers, writers and management what had happened. From there, the news-gathering machinery started to grind out all the details of the assassination. I worked almost 36 hours straight without a break, and the full realization of what had happened did not hit me until two days after those shots rang out in Dallas. But whenever anyone mentions that day, it all flashes back as a vivid recollection of something I shall never forget as long as I live.

GORDON HOWE, *professional ice hockey player*

**HARTFORD
WHALERS**
Hockey Club

One Civic Center Plaza
Hartford, Connecticut 06103
(203) 728-3366

April 27, 1983

Mrs. Jodie Elliott Hansen
Box 1031
Union City, TN 38261

Dear Mrs. Hansen:

The day President John F. Kennedy was assassinated, I recall entering
my car to head home after our daily hockey practice in the Olympia
Stadium in Detroit, as a member of the Red Wings.

The news hit me like I had been shot myself. The first thing I did
was call home to relay the terrible news, only to have my wife
Colleen answer with tears, she had heard the news last. The next
move I recall was to run back into the dressing room to let my
teammates know of the bad news.

The rest of the day was spent with our ears and eyes glued to the
news in hopes that our prayers would be answered and good news
would come our way. The news we received is history now. I hope
and pray the price this great man paid will never have to be paid
by anyone again.

Kindest regards,

Gordon Howe

Gordon Howe

HARTFORD WHALERS HOCKEY CLUB

GH:ljt

SARAH T. HUGHES, U.S. District Court Judge, conducted President Lyndon Johnson's swearing-in

THE PRESIDENT IS SWORN IN

By SARAH T. HUGHES
United States District Judge for
the Northern District of Texas

It was 2:15, Friday, November 22. I had just reached home from the Trade Mart, where a large and enthusiastic crowd had gathered to see and hear President John F. Kennedy. We waited in vain, for he had been assassinated as he was leaving the downtown area of Dallas.

Numbed and hardly realizing what had happened, I drove home. There was no reason to go to court. In the face of the tragedy that had befallen us, all else seemed of little consequence.

I phoned the court to tell the clerk where I was. Her response was that Barefoot Sanders, U. S. attorney, wanted to speak to me. Immediately I heard his familiar voice, "The Vice-President wants you to swear him in as President. Can you do it? How soon can you get to the airport?" Of course I could, and I could be there in ten minutes.

I got in my car and started toward the airport. Now there was another job to be done - a new President who had to carry on, and he must qualify for the office as quickly as possible. He had much to do, and I must think of him, and do the job that had been assigned to me.

There was no time to find the oath administered to a president, but the essentials of every oath are the same. You have to swear to perform the duties of the office of the President of the United States, and to preserve and defend the Constitution of the United States. I was not afraid. I could do it without a formal oath.

Police blocked the entrance to the location of the plane, but there was no difficulty. They knew me, and I told them I was there to swear in the Vice-President as President. One of the motorcycle officers went to the plane to confirm my statement and then escorted me to the plane.

(continued)

It was a beautiful sight, the presidential plane, long and sleek, a blue and two white stripes running the length of the plane, with the words, "The United States of America," on the blue stripe. It seemed to exemplify the strength and courage of our country.

I was escorted up the ramp by the chief of police to the front door, where one of the Vice-President's aides and the Secret Service met me. I was trying to explain that I did not have the presidential oath but could give it anyway when someone handed me a copy.

In the second compartment were several Texas congressmen, vice-presidential aides, Secret Service men, and the Vice-President and Mrs. Johnson. Mr. and Mrs. Johnson have been my friends for many years, but on such an occasion, there did not seem to be anything to say. I embraced them both, for that was the best way to give expression to my feeling of grief for them, and for all of us.

By that time a Bible that was on the plane had been thrust into my hands. It was a small volume, with soft leather backs. I thought someone said it was a Catholic Bible. I do not know, but I would like to think it was, and that President Kennedy had been reading it on this, his last trip.

The Vice-President said Mrs. Kennedy wanted to be present for the ceremony, and in a very few minutes she appeared. Her face showed her grief, but she was composed and calm. She, too, exemplified the courage this country needs to carry on. The Vice-President leaned toward her and told her I was a U. S. judge appointed by her husband. My acknowledgement was, "I loved him very much."

The Vice-President asked Mrs. Johnson to stand on his right, Mrs. Kennedy on his left, and with his hand on the Bible, slowly and reverently repeated the oath after me: "I do solemnly swear that I will perform the duties of President of the United States to the best of my ability and defend, protect, and preserve the Constitution of the United States." That was all to the oath I had in my hand, but I added, "So help me God," and he said it after me. It seemed that that needed to be said.

He gently kissed Mrs. Kennedy and leaned over and kissed his wife on the cheek.

Here was a man with the ability and determination for the task ahead. Great as are the responsibilities of the office, I felt he could carry on. I told him so, and that we were behind him, and he would have our sympathy and our help.

As I left the plane I heard him give the order to take off, "Now let's get ready and go." I drove away with my thoughts on this man, upon whom so much now depended.

Sarah T. Hughes

E. HOWARD HUNT

I was driving with my wife and 2-month-old son in downtown Washington when I heard the news of JFK's shooting on the car radio. I felt physically nauseated, then angered when Chet Huntley speculated with some conviction that right-wing fanatics were responsible,and one could expect no less in a city(Dallas) where Adlai Stevenson once had been spat upon. Amid rumprs of a coup d'etat I felt
                                three
deep concern for my/school-age children,and we set off to collect them from their schools and take them to the security of our home.

1245 N.E. 85 Street, Miami, FL 33138

JAMES B. IRWIN, *astronaut*

HIGH FLIGHT FOUNDATION

202 E. Cheyenne Mountain Blvd. • P.O. Box 1387 • Colorado Springs, Colorado 80901
(303) 576-7700

May 28, 1981

Mrs. Jodie Elliott Hansen
Box 1031
Union City, Tennessee 38261

Dear Mrs. Hansen,

Thank you for the opportunity to contribute my memories
to the many thousands of other memories you have collected
from that very sad day.

It happened when I was serving as test pilot at Edwards
AFB. I was alone when I learned the news from the radio.
I was stunned as if I had been hit. I wondered, "Can this
really be true?" It wasn't very long until I realized I
had lost a great president. There was sadness all around
me, and the days' activities came to a standstill.

President Kennedy was a great president. It is a tragedy
that he could not have lived to see us reach the goal he
established in 1962 - "We shall send man to the moon in
this decade and return him safely to the earth."

Your friend from space,

James B. Irwin
President

JBI/kd

"Man's flight through life is sustained by the power of *His* knowledge."

T. H. IRWIN *(in 1963) resident of Ireland*

I was shaving and about to go out to a local "hop" when the TV programme (a quiz show as I remember) was interrupted to inform us that shots had been fired at JFK during a visit to Dallas. That was quite a bombshell but it wasn't considered all that serious as we were not even told that he had been hit. The big trauma came about a half-hour later when a special news broadcast came on the air with the opening shock that "President Kennedy is dead!" That was a helluva thing to try to take in and I recall that my immediate fear was that a negro might have done it with the obvious reactions.... When JFK was elected there was much celebration of him being "the first Irish President." Of course the Republic of Ireland made a big thing of this and his visit here in 1963 was the zenith. Being very aware of American History and the contribution made by my fellow Scotch-Irish it would have been more honest to say that Kennedy was "the first Roman Catholic President." It was, and seems to always be, conveniently forgotten that the following Presidents were of direct Scotch-Irish ancestry (and therefore Protestant Irish): Andrew Jackson, James Polk, James Buchanan, Andrew Johnson, Ulysses S. Grant, Chester Arthur, Grover Cleveland, Benjamin Harrison, William McKinley, and Woodrow Wilson....How about that for a small beleaguered province of only 1,500,000 people?

"COTTON IVY," *(in 1963) country humorist, politician*

My family and I were on the way to the doctor's when we heard the news over the radio. We contemplated turning around and going back home. Why home? Home meant security, reassurance. At that moment we needed these things. But we kept our appointment even though our illnesses seemed secondary right then.

President Kennedy died that day and a little bit of me died with him. I am sure many other Americans felt the same. I was so saddened that day and twenty-five years later I am still saddened by his death.

I was born and raised in a family that believed the Democratic party was the only party. We were democrats "Southern style." My daddy right now has pictures of Presidents Roosevelt and Kennedy right next to one of our Lord. He says proudly, "There are three real democrats—ain't they?" He votes the straight ticket and can't understand why one of his children would vote independent.

J.F.K. was revered around our country in spite of him being a Catholic and talking "funny." We honored him as president of our country. I related to what he was and what he did. The assassination of the president was like losing a close friend that I could trust. First anger hit me—anger toward the man who had killed our president. Then pity engulfed me for the assassin as well as the Kennedy family. What will America do without this good man and great leader, I thought.

LEO JAFFE
711 FIFTH AVENUE
NEW YORK

Mrs Jodie Hansen,

Re Ur letter of April 29th I recall most vividly that I was having lunch at the N.Y.U. Alumni Club with a partner of Merrill Lynch, when a messenger came to our table and advised me I was wanted on the phone for an urgent call.

I left my table and went to the phone. My Secretary was on the line and told me she had just heard a flash report that the President had been Shot. No details were available, but he was being rushed to a hospital in Dallas

Needless to say, We Stopped our

luncheon and quickly returned to our respective offices to listen to reports, which were ominous, with great confusion in evidence, until we heard the report shortly thereafter that our President was dead.

It was hard to believe — I was in shock along with everyone else — shed tears and was heartsick.

I knew the President, had dined with him on several occasions, and couldn't fully realize for quite some time that it was over — he was dead — that the Country and every Citizen lost a great friend and leader.

I ordered our offices to be closed immediately, went home and sat glued to the television for the balance of the afternoon and night, along with my wife.

That my recollection

Sincerely, Les Jaffe

21 Richter Ave
Milltown, N J 08850
Jan 4, 1979

Elliot Enterprises
P O Box 1031
Union City, Tenn 38261

On the day and hour of JFK's assassination, I was sitting in my office writing a letter to John McGuire of Jacksonville Fla. John was Radioman on JFK's PT 109 when it was rammed by a Jap Ship.

John joined my Squadron after being rescued and we became good friends I was writing to him to make arrangements for the two of us to meet at Palm Beach, Fla at a time when the President would be there. He wanted me to meet the President.

The sad news from Dallas, changed my entire letter to a letter of Condolence

Very Truly
Walter Jensen
P.T. Ron 7
RM 1/c

MAX JONES *(in 1963) flight chief with 90th Tactical Fighter Squadron at Misawa Air Base, Japan*

It was 9:30 A.M., Saturday November 23, 1963, in Japan and I was at the NCO club, playing shuffleboard and drinking beer with several others. We were surprised when the alert system was activated—three long blasts. The wing commander told all personnel to report to duty sections immediately.

We did not know, at that time, the reason for the alarm. It was then that the squadron commander said very slowly and in a grave manner that the President of the United States had been shot in Dallas. It seemed like forever before anyone made a sound.

Lieutenant Colonel White then instructed us emphatically to not discuss the news with anyone, not among ourselves, and especially not with any Japanese officials. We were released to return to our living quarters, and instructed to remain on stand-by notice.

A short time thereafter, we were recalled back to the duty section and told to get the 6F 100 fighters ready for "upload" (loaded with six 600-lb bombs and four missiles)....On Tuesday around twelve noon, there was a full military formation along with a memorial service held simultaneously with a flyover. The American flag was at half-mast. The Japanese flew six F-86 planes over the base backed up by the American planes—six 100s, six 101s, and six 105s, as a solemn tribute to the dead chief of state.

NAOMI JONES *(in 1963) business manager in Memphis, Tennessee*

Every time I hear or read anything about the Kennedy assassination I think of a traumatic incident my second cousin experienced. This young man was 18–20 at the time and was working in Dallas in the vicinity of the assassination site. Hearing all the commotion and not knowing what had happened, he and two of his co-workers ran out into the street, over the railroad tracks, and away from the scene of the crime—although they did not even know there had been a crime. They were picked up by policemen, taken to jail as suspects, and were kept there all afternoon and all night. His sister was married to a man from one of the most prominent and influential families in Dallas. They pulled every string they could to have him released from jail but were unsuccessful until the following morning.

THE UNIVERSITY OF TEXAS AT AUSTIN
LYNDON B. JOHNSON SCHOOL OF PUBLIC AFFAIRS
AUSTIN, TEXAS 78712

(512)-471-4962

August 28, 1981

Jodie Elliott Hansen
Box 1031
Union City, TN 38261

Dear Mrs. Hansen:

I have received your letter of July 30. My memories regarding
that fateful day remain too personal for me to share them
with others. I'm sorry.

Good luck in your compilation.

Sincerely yours,

Barbara Jordan

BJ/lr

BIL KEANE, *syndicated cartoonist, creator of* Family Circus

5815 E. Joshua Tree Lane, Paradise Valley, Arizona 85253

May 16, 1982

Dear Jodie,

ENCLOSED IS MY ACCOUNT
OF MY PERSONAL EXPERIENCE
OF THE KENNEDY ASSASSINATION.
SOUNDS LIKE AN INTERESTING,
INTRIGUING PROJECT. GOOD
LUCK WITH THE BOOK. THANK
YOU FOR INCLUDING ME.
BEST WISHES FROM THE
FAMILY CIRCUS!

SINCERELY,

BIL KEANE

On that morning in peaceful Paradise Valley, Arizona, I was as usual
at the drawing board in my home studio drawing a "Family Circus" cartoon.
My wife opened the door and said they had interrupted "Password" on TV
with a news bulletin that President Kennedy had been shot in Dallas. I
switched on the television set in my studio and was launched into the nightmare
of progressive reports that built to the unbelievable climax: John F. Kennedy
was dead.

Concentrating on drawing a humorous, light-hearted portrayal of typical
American family life was almost impossible. Work was put aside. The
single topic of the assassination pervaded every thought, every conversation
from that moment on, reaching a bizarre peak a few days later when I witnessed
the only "live" killing in my life when Lee Harvey Oswald was shot by Jack
Ruby in front of the TV cameras.

Bil Keane

BOB KEESHAN, *television entertainer, "Captain Kangaroo"*

We were in our television studio rehearsing our next show. I asked Timo, our stage manager, a question. From fifteen feet away, alongside a camera, he was staring into space his face showing complete bewilderment. I repeated my question and in response he rushed toward me pulling the earpiece from his communication gear. I was dumbfounded as he shoved the earpiece into <u>my</u> ear and then I listened. It was Walter Cronkite breaking the news. Was he dead? We did not think so. And then, shortly, we learned the complete, incomprehensible truth. Almost no words were spoken as forty people, actors, production personnel, stagehands, technicians immediately left the studio and the building to go to their homes to join the rest of the nation in mourning.

BOB KEESHAN/CAPTAIN KANGAROO

GRACE KELLY, *Princess Consort of Monaco*

LE CHEF DU SECRÉTARIAT
DE
S.A.S.LA PRINCESSE DE MONACO

August 23, 1979

Dear Mrs. Hansen,

H.S.H. Princess Grace has asked me to answer your kind letter of August 2, 1979 and to give you the following details on how She heard the news of the assassination of the late President John F. Kennedy:

Because of the six hours difference of time with the United States, the Princess first heard of the shooting in the evening when She was putting Her children to bed.

H.S.H. Prince Rainier came rushing into the nursery to tell Her what He had just heard on TV. Then, They both went out to see Prince Rainier's father, H.S.H. Prince Pierre, to tell Him the news. They were all shocked but they thought at the time that it was only an attempt to kill the President, as not many details had been given on TV.

It was only later on in the evening that They knew it had been a fatal shooting and that President Kennedy was dead.

Sincerely yours,

P. Choisit

Paul Choisit

United States Senate
WASHINGTON, D.C. 20510

July 19, 1979

Mrs. Jodie Hansen
Box 1031
Union City, Tennessee 38261

Dear Mrs. Hansen:

My family has been aware of various theories concerning the death of President Kennedy, just as it has been aware of the many speculative accounts which have arisen from the death of Robert Kennedy.

I am sure that it is understood that the continual speculation is painful for members of my family. Our feeling is that, if there is sufficient evidence to re-examine the circumstances concerning the deaths of President Kennedy and Robert Kennedy, this judgment would have to be made by the legal authorities responsible for such further examination. I do not believe that their judgment should be influenced by any feelings or discomfort by any member of my family.

Sincerely,

Edward M. Kennedy

DEBORAH KERR, *actress*

Los Monteros,
Marbella,
Malaga,
Spain.

July 20th. 1982.

Dear Mrs Hansen,

Thank you for your letter requesting what my reactions were to the assassination of President Kennedy.

I was in Puerto Vallarta, Mexico, making the movie "Night Of The Iguana" with Richard Burton and Ava Gardner. We happened to be shooting at night, so I did not leave the house until late afternoon, to go to the beach where a small speed-boat would take one or two of us across the bay to the location.

My husband, Peter Viertel, had already gone to the beach for a swim, and when I arrived by car he said, as I got out, "They've shot the President." I honestly thought he meant the President of Mexico, and I said relatively unemotionally, "Oh dear! How dreadful!" Peter saw I didn't realize, and said "President Kennedy." I was completely stunned. I could not <u>believe</u> him. There was an air of total unreality as we boarded the boat and set off. Nobody spoke at <u>all</u>, except an occasional 'My God.'

On arrival at the location there was the same stunned atmosphere, and none of us could get going with our preparations for the night's work - hair - make-up etc. etc. Finally, of course, we did. Work had to go on. I remember before we began rehearsing, John Huston, the director, called for everyone to join in two minutes silence. It was too staggering and too <u>unreal</u> to cry. One just felt a heavy load on one's heart. Later of course we were glued to our radio sets and, reception from the States being very poor, it was dreadfully frustrating. Finally, of course, all the details sifted through; and it has always seemed to me that with his tragic assassination, the flood-gates of violence were opened, and since then the world has been deluged with more and more killing and violence. Where will it all lead?

I hope my recollection of this unforgettable day will be of use in your book.

With kindest regards,

Deborah Kerr Viertel.

<u>Deborah</u> <u>Kerr</u> <u>Viertel</u>.

HANK KETCHAM, *syndicated cartoonist, creator of* Dennis the Menace

Hank Ketcham
Enterprises, Inc
P.O. Box 800, Pebble Beach, Calif. 93953
(408) 625-3130

25 September 1981

Dear Mrs. Hansen:

I am enclosing a rather belated response to your request dated August 3rd concerning "memories of the day President John Kennedy was assassinated". It all seems like so very long ago, doesn't it?

I wish you the best of luck in this imaginative publishing effort and look forward to seeing a copy in our neighborhood book store. This should add an unusual personal perspective to this shocking turn of events.

Cordially,

H. Ketcham

Mrs. Jodie Elliott Hansen
P. O. Box 1031
Union City, Tennessee 38261

HKK:dwr
Enclosure

AS I REMEMBER IT

Political jokes are always in season, so I gave little thought to a one-liner from a friend concerning "our new President, Lyndon B. Johnson". In fact, I didn't understand the remark and asked for a replay, and then was informed of the tragedy which had taken place within the hour.

It was a warm summer evening in Geneva, Switzerland and I, like everyone in the western world, was totally unprepared for this blockbuster and first reaction was utter disbelief. A cruel joke. A huge mistake or another diabolical rumor. Of course, the news was pouring out of radios all over town in a wide variety of languages and the / Voice Of America quickly affirmed the horrible truth to we yankees whose vocabularies in French or German were limited. I spent the balance of the evening with a few close expatriot pals, alternately sipping whiskey, shaking our heads and summoning up as much philosophy as we could muster. We felt a bit like a crew without a skipper.

During the days following, I was regularly stopped on the street by complete strangers, Swiss, Italian and German, each one anxious to offer condolence and to convey their personal sense of shock and loss directly to an American. It was a touching experience and seemed to underscore the immense wave of world wide popularity which this young President engendered in such a brief period.

Henry K. Ketcham, 9-25-81.

EDWARD I. KOCH, *Mayor of New York City*

THE CITY OF NEW YORK
OFFICE OF THE MAYOR
NEW YORK, N.Y. 10007

May 7, 1979

Mrs. Jodie Hansen
Box 1031
Union City, Tenn.   38261

Dear Mrs. Hansen:

I have your letter of April 27, 1979.

On January 22, 1963, I was in my law office and was
told by a colleague that President Kennedy had been shot
and was dying. I remember bursting into tears and
suffering inconsolable pain and rage all weekend long.
It was as though a member of my immediate family had been
the victim.

Sincerely,

Edward I. Koch
Mayor

mg

JOSEPH E. KUCHARSKI *(in 1963) resident of Detroit, Michigan*

I was told the tragic news by a waitress while having lunch at Carl's Chop House in Detroit. A salesman friend was with me and we thought it was a joke—a sick joke. I also recall being on Grand River Avenue when they announced he was dead. My friend and neighbor, Don Ephlin, who was from the Boston area and involved in union politics, was very hurt and actually went into mourning. I am a Catholic but did not vote for JFK for this reason. I voted for him because of his charisma and public relations talents. I think it is of the upmost importance for any public figure to make the people feel he is a part of them and to instill confidence. To travel and mix with the people is very important for the personal contact—so that they can say, "I saw him, I met him, I touched him . . ." I'm a bit fuzzy with my memories of JFK—my true memories. I've read many books about the man and the assassination and feel that I, along with many others, cannot be completely honest and objective because reality might be somewhat distorted from what we've read or heard in the past 16 years.

dallas cowboys football club

May 5, 1980

Mrs. Jodie Elliott Hansen
Box 1031
Union City, Tennessee   38261

Dear Mrs. Hansen:

You requested a comment or two concerning my memory of
where I was when I heard the news of the assassination
of the late president, John J. Kennedy. I remember the
occasion very vividly.

We were on the practice field with the Dallas Cowboys,
preparing for a game against the Cleveland Browns. Someone brought the news to the sideline and one of our trainers
came on the field and told me what had happened. Of course
we were all in shock and I called practice off at that
moment.

It's always a sad day when something tragic happens and
especially when it happens right in your own home town.
I am sure that almost everybody felt as I did at that
moment.

I hope these comments will help you in your preparation
for your book.

Sincerely yours,

Tom Landry
Head Coach

TL:mk

WALTER LANTZ, *animator, creator of* Woody Woodpecker

PRODUCTIONS, INC.

WALTER LANTZ
PRESIDENT

TELEVISION CENTER
6311 ROMAINE STREET · HOLLYWOOD, CA 90038
PHONE (213) 469-2907

January 31, 1983

Mrs. Jodie Elliott Hansen
Box 1031
Union City, TN   38261

RE: The assassination
of President John
Kennedy

Dear Mrs. Hansen:

At the time of the incident captioned above, I was
in New York having an interview with an Associated
Press writer in Sardi's Restaurant. Suddenly, it
seemed like panic started. People stopped eating and
rushed to telephones.

The writer and I couldn't imagine what had happened,
and then the word came that President Kennedy had
been assassinated!

I went outside, and people were in a state of shock.
They were talking and crying, and just could not
believe that our President had been assassinated.

Even to this day, I find it difficult to think about
the tragedy.

Sincerely,

Walter Lantz

Walter Lantz

WL:dbl

GORDON LAWHEAD *(in 1963) ad salesman at RKO General in New York City*

As I was crossing Fifth Avenue I noticed a large crowd gathered in front of a television retail sales outlet store. I knew there was special news on because it was an unusual time of the day for the well-known commentators (Uncle Walter, Brinkley, etc.) to be on. The people were watching the TV sets through the store windows but could not hear what the commentators were saying. A deaf lady in the crowd read the lips of the newsmen and told the people around her the President had been shot. Needless to say, there was shock and disbelief among the people in the crowd. I returned to the office and immediately received word to notify all stations and sponsors that no commercials would be run until further notice, although many of the sponsors had already called to cancel their commercials. There were none shown until after the President's funeral.

To   Mrs. Jodie Elliott Hansen

From Art Linkletter

May 10,1979

Dear Mrs. Hansen:

I am replying to your letter of the 5th
to Mr. Linkletter, as he departed this
morning for Europe and will not return
for 6 to 8 weeks.

However, I was with Mr. Linkletter at
CBS Television City the day President
Kennedy was assassinated so know what
he was doing, namely, he and our staff
and CBS crew were taping HOUSE PARTY
shows. The news was heard in the control
booth by our director (or assistant director; can't recall) that Mr. Kennedy
"appeared to have been shot." It was
over an hour before it was determined
that he had been shot perhaps fatally.
When our taping session finished, Mr.
Linkletter told our live audience that
they should go to the nearest radio,
their automobiles in most cases, and
listen for further news of the shooting.
Mr. Linkletter and his staff remained
at the studio until we learned via a
CBS monitor that the President's wounds
were fatal. I don't think even one of
us bothered to go on to lunch that day.

Cordially,   Secretary

Henry Cabot Lodge

Beverly, Massachusetts
September 29, 1980

Mrs. Jodie Elliott Hansen
Box 1031
Union City, Tennessee 38261

Dear Mrs. Hansen:

      This is in reply to your letter
of September 15 asking me what I was doing
at the time of the assassination of President
Kennedy. My answer is:

      I was on my way home from my post
in Viet Nam and had flown across the Pacific
and gone to bed in the St. Francis Hotel. I
was just having breakfast in my room when the
manager of the hotel called me telling me of
the President's assassination. I was, of course,
shocked. *profoundly*

      President Kennedy had sent for me
to come to Washington for a conference with him
about Viet Nam. I was on my way there. I was
told to continue my trip to Washington and later
on in the day I had a conference with President
Johnson.

Sincerely yours,

Henry Cabot Lodge

LORETTA LYNN, *country music entertainer*

Loretta Lynn
Enterprises, Inc.

7 Music Circle North
Nashville, Tennessee 37203

April 8, 1981

Mrs Jodie Elliott Hansen
Box 1031
Union City, Tn 38261

Dear Mrs Hansen:

I am sorry to be so long in answering your letter of March 3,
addressed to Loretta but I only recently had the chance to
discuss it with her.

Loretta's statement regarding President Kennedy's assassination
is as follows:

> "My husband and I and some other Country Music artists
> were in Dallas at the time we heard that the President
> had been shot. We were on our way to Albequerque, New
> Mexico to do a show that night. We kept our car radio
> on and learned the news of his death.
>
> Our car was the first one in the group traveling to-
> gether and my husband pulled over to the side of the
> road and the others did too. He told all the rest of
> them what we had just heard. As for me, I couldn't
> talk for crying.
>
> When we got to Albequerque we wondered whether we should
> do the show. The men in charge of the show talked to
> the audience and even though lots of people were crying
> we decided to go ahead and do the show.
>
> When the show was over all of us sat around and talked
> and just couldn't believe it had happened. I thought
> so much of President Kennedy that I couldn't sleep that
> night. I just kept on watching television and decided
> that things had to go on without him."

(615) 259-2021

CHARLES HABIB MALIK, *Lebanese philosopher and diplomat*

Charles Habib Malik

The Representative, Apartment 715
1101 South Arlington Ridge Road
Arlington, Virginia 22202

May 18, 1982

Mrs. Jodie Elliott Hansen
Box 1031
Union City, Tennessee 38261

Dear Mrs. Hansen:

Thank you for your letter of May 3, 1982 and its enclosures. In 1963 at the moment when President Kennedy was assassinated I was sitting in our house in Lebanon reading the Bible. I shut myself up in my study meditating on some Psalms. All of a sudden my mother-in-law pounded the door with unusual vigor. I realized something must be amiss. I said, "Come in." She opened the door and told me that she had just heard on the radio that President Kennedy was shot but there was no news yet that he was killed. Shortly thereafter my wife, my son and many friends and relatives gathered together in our house fully aghast at what had happened. We could do nothing but keep listening on the radio as to whether President Kennedy was still alive. I think it was a couple of hours before the announcement came that after taking him to the hospital the doctors could not revive him and he was pronounced dead. We spent hours afterwards contemplating the tragedy and discussing its significance from every angle. A few days afterwards a special memorial service for President Kennedy was held at the American University of Beirut where I was a professor and I was asked to give the memorial address. My address was later chosen to be included in a volume issued by the White House containing a selection of speeches and statements made about the tragic event all over the world. Some of my feelings I poured in that statement.

Faithfully yours,

March 14, 1981

Dear Jodie:

Thank you so much for your letter and for asking me to
participate in the book you are planning to write. It
sounds like it will be a fascinating book and I'd be more
than delighted to be a part of it.

At the time of John Kennedy's assassination I was at the
studio rehearsing the Dick van Dyke show. The prop man
came onto the set (he had been listening to his radio back-
stage) and told us the President had just been shot. At
first we didn't believe him - told him it wasn't funny and
we didn't need a joke like that in the script. We all stopped
rehearsing when he convinced us that it was true and we ran
to the prop room to hear further details. When word came that
he was dead all of us started crying. I immediately went to
a phone and called my husband. He was home sleeping and when
I told him to turn on the T.V. he was in shock. He too thought
I had been kidding.

Rehearsal was naturally called off for the rest of the day and
we all quietly left the studio. I got into my car and drove
home - crying all the way.

My husband and I sat glued to the television set for two days.
We finally decided to try and redecorate our guest room as a
way to stop watching the very sad events that had been taking
place over the past several days.

Thank you again for having written to me Jodie and I wish you
much good luck with your book.

Blessings to you always.

All love and appreciation,

RM/dw

S. M. MATARAZZO *(in 1963) high school principal for military dependents at Fort Knox, Kentucky*

I remember that while absorbing the shock of JFK's death and the drama of the subsequent weekend events, my thoughts and observations were on the previous presidential assassinations in the history of our country (Lincoln, Garfield, and McKinley). I was feeling a personal loss in regard to the death of JFK, but I felt confident that our country would weather this storm, just as it had previously. I was very much aware of the intricate mechanisms of our system and how the government would function well and that the transitional processes were in motion immediately. Comparing this tragedy with the death of President Lincoln, had there been the instant communications system then as we had in 1963, there would have been problems of monumental proportion, because of the heated passions of the times concerning the Civil War, the division of the country, and the struggles of the Reconstruction. I remember thinking that in a dictatorship, an assassination of this type would have incited utter chaos with tremendous repercussions.

WALTER MATTHAU, *actor*

NIVERSAL CITY STUDIOS, INC., 100 UNIVERSAL CITY PLAZA, UNIVERSAL CITY, CA. 91608, 213-985-4321

February 21, 1980

Mrs. Jodie Elliott Hansen
Box 1031
Union City, Tennessee 38261

Dear Mrs. Hansen:

A friend of mine called me with the
news that President Kennedy had been shot.
I then turned on the television set and
just stared at it until the news came
that he was dead.

My friend showed up at the house and
we drank three quarts of 100 proof vodka in
the next six hours and I don't drink!

Sincerely,

Walter Matthau

WM/g

SARAH McCLENDON

2933 28th Street, N.W., Washington, D.C. 20008

News Correspondent and Columnist • Radio-TV Newscaster • Lecturer • Consultant
McClendon News Service • Texas Trends • White House Reports

(202) 483-3719
483-7918

December 6, 1982

Dear Jodie,

    I remember vividly the phone call from a blind friend that interrupted my work in my office to tell me the shocking news of Kennedy's death. I was on the White House porch when he turned around and waved to the reporters when he left for Dallas. I immediately left for the airport to await the arrival of the casket. -- Jackie in her blood-stained suit and Evelyn Lincoln immaculate in her white gloves. I was touched to see Jackie get into the front seat of the hearse that carried th body. Later, I remember the press corps walking behind the casket all the way from the White House to the Capitol where he laid in state.

    It was such a sad occasion for all of us.

Sincerely,

Sarah McClendon

Larry T. McGehee *(in 1963) Ph.D. student at Yale University*

I watched him (JFK) at the 1960 convention and thought he was too brash, too rich, too young—and Mrs. Roosevelt and Senator Eugene McCarthy convinced me Adlai Stevenson was the man for the times. I didn't take much convincing, because I believed then in the power of words, and Adlai held me by my ears in 1960 as he had in 1952 and 1956. Sometime between the convention and the election I became a convert, and Kennedy held my eyes, remarkable for his ease before television or still cameras. By the time of the Kennedy-Nixon debates, I was hooked.

By Inauguration Day—when he proved he could do as well as Stevenson in a formal speech—I was so converted that I had lost all sense of objectivity, and was quite willing to forgive him his father, his wooden wife, his money, his Boston accent, his Harvard degree, his selection of Lyndon Johnson as a running mate, and his abundant hair.

Television brought him to us, and we found substance behind the image—and the substance was his dreams. He lacked the practical politics he needed, since his election majority was so slim and his congressional party support so scant, so he gave us something better: blueprints, challenge, statements of needs and of goals for a better world, a better nation, and better persons.

(continued)

I don't remember leaving there (the television lounge) for two or three days, until Jack Ruby had killed Oswald. I watched everything they televised, every replay they showed. There was never any sense of disbelief— television made it too clear that it had happened, and thereby probably served the nation better than TV ever has. I remember, too, the one precise moment in all that coverage when I finally wept. Not when John-John saluted or when Mike Mansfield spoke or when the crowd filed so silently by the casket or when the world's leaders walked together down the Avenue. It was that moment at Arlington when the flag was removed and folded, and a black man in the honor guard took the triangle to Mrs. Kennedy. It was the symbolism of a black man doing it that grabbed my inside and summed up so many emotions and summoned up my tears.

WILLIAM J. MCGILL, *president, Columbia University*

Columbia University
in the City of New York

NEW YORK, N.Y. 10027

PRESIDENT'S ROOM

March 18, 1980

Dear Mrs. Hansen:

On November 22, 1963 I was working in an office at Stanford in Palo Alto where I was visiting on leave from Columbia for a year. My wife heard a news flash on the radio as she was cleaning our house on Bryant Street. We had rented it for the year. She rushed to the telephone to call me in Ventura Hall at Stanford.

When she got through it was about 10:30 a.m. and she was in tears. The department secretary who received the call asked her what was wrong. My wife said, "The President has been shot." The secretary could not believe it. "That is impossible, I saw President Sterling not more than half an hour ago." My wife replied, "Migod you fool I am talking about the President of the United States!"

I went home immediately and we held hands watching Walter Cronkite in his shirt sleeves on TV as he read the medical bulletins from Dallas. We saw him falter and listened to his voice break as he reported that President Kennedy was dead.

Sincerely,

William J. McGill
President

Mrs. Jodie Elliott Hansen
Box 1031
Union City, Tennessee 38261

hg/t

The Washington Star

225 Virginia Avenue, S.E.

Washington, D.C. 20061

Mary McGrory

January 2, 1980

Mrs. Jodie Elliott Hansen
Box 1031
803 Exchange Street
Union City, Tennessee   38261

Dear Mrs. Hansen:

Thank you for your letter of so long ago. I do not envy
you your task.

I was at a doctor's office having my blood pressure taken
at the fateful moment. The doctor was very concerned and said
he had just heard a rumor that "Kennedy had been shot down." I
thought it meant his plane had been attacked.

On my way to the office, I heard on the cab's radio what
had actually taken place. The newsroom of The Star was crowded.
The national editor said, "We want you to go to Dallas" and he
stuffed a wad of bills into my hand. A few minutes later, I
sought him out and said, "What if Kennedy dies?" At approximately
that moment, Walter Cronkite told us he was dead. I worked all
weekend. I went to the airport to see the body brought home.
I went to the White House for the wake. I went to the Capitol
to see the public homage and stood in line for much of that Sunday
night while people waited for hours to file past and played guitars
and sang and were nice to one another. I went to the funeral
and rode back from Arlington with the Australian Ambassador. I
wrote every day and was grateful I had something to do.

Happy New Year.

Sincerely,

Mary McGrory

Mary McGrory

KINNAIRD MCKEE, *U.S. Navy Vice Admiral*

Commander THIRD Fleet
Pearl Harbor, Hawaii 96860

6 July 1979

Dear Mrs. Hansen,

Congratulations on your very interesting John F. Kennedy project. It seems from your letter of June 10 that you've compiled some noteworthy memoirs of people responding to the loss of our late president.

At the time of John Kennedy's death I was executive officer of the 410-foot fleet ballistic missile submarine SAM HOUSTON. Our "gold" crew of 142 sailormen had been on HOUSTON's sixth deterrent patrol in the North Atlantic.

Upon our return to homeport in Holy Loch, Scotland word of the assissination of the President, although late, stunned all of us onboard.

Unfortunately I did not keep any newspaper clips or other memorabilia about President Kennedy or the assissination. By the time our ship pulled back into port the immediate shock of the public had subsided.

Wishing you every success with your book.

Sincerely,

KINNAIRD R. McKEE
Vice Admiral, U. S. Navy

Mrs. Jodie Elliot Hansen
Box 1031
Union City, TN 38261

Feb. 3, 1980

Dear Mrs. Hansen,

I was on a plane to be the guest speaker for the Wisconsin state democratic rally when the announcements first broke and had still not heard anything until I got in the cab in Milwaukee. The cab driver turned to me and said, "Did you hear that Kennedy was shot?"

Since I had heard every Kennedy joke there was for 2 years I said, "No, how does it go?"

Needless to say, it was no joke. The rally was cancelled and I took the next plane home.

Your book sounds most interesting. I shall look forward to seeing it on the stands.

Sincerely,

Vaughn Meader

KARL, MENNINGER, M.D., *psychiatrist, founder of the Menninger Foundation and Clinic*

The Menninger Foundation

BOX 829   TOPEKA, KANSAS 66601   913/234-9566

March 20, 1980

Mrs. Jodie Elliott Hansen
Box 1031
Union City, Tennessee 38261

Dear Mrs. Hansen:

Thank you for your letter of March 12, asking form my comments on what my memories were and the feelings I had about the assassination of the late President Kennedy.

I remember exactly where I was. I was standing in the outer doorway of my secretary's office, just entering. She hastily told me the news (I don't know how she got it.) and I was incredulous, frightened, horror stricken. I thought of the dismay that the news was bringing to millions, especially to those who adored him as I did. I was more shaken than on the day of the news of Pearl Harbor, which I also remember clearly. I don't think my secretary or I had any intelligent, constructive thoughts or comments. Gradually, we remembered various (earlier) menacing news items from Dallas.

Then I saw that shocking television newscast in which Ruby shot Oswald, just while we were trying to catch Oswald's words as he was being led into jail. It happened so fast and so absurdly and so senselessly that I could scarcely believe it to be real. The whole thing seems like a nightmare. But it was on television like a show. We have almost forgotten it but it is still disturb-ing.

You are doing a good think, I believe, to remind us.

Sincerely,

Karl Menninger, M.D., M.A.C.P.

KM/lf

Y ᴇ ʜ ᴜ ᴅ ɪ M ᴇ ɴ ᴜ ʜ ɪ ɴ, *classical violinist*

15 POND SQUARE
HIGHGATE VILLAGE
LONDON N6 6BA   17th March 1982

Dear Mrs Hansen

On the day that President Kennedy was
assassinated, I was playing a concert
with the Minneapolis Symphony Orchestra
and Stanislaw Skrowaczewski. We were
deeply shocked to learn the news, and
I went on to the stage to play the
Chaconne from the D minor Partita of
Bach as a tribute to the memory of
the President.

                    Yours sincerely,

                    [signature]

                    Yehudi Menuhin

LEWIS MILLETT *(in 1963) Lieutenant Colonel in the military, college student in Parkville, Missouri*

I was with a group of servicemen at the time and their conversation and discussion centered on the assumption that the assassin was a right-wing kook or an anarchist, and even the possibility that he might be involved with the KKK. Later, when discovering that Lee Harvey Oswald was just the opposite, it amazed me that a former Marine married the daughter of a KGB Colonel, because the Russians just do not allow things like that unless it is to their benefit.

FRED MONTGOMERY *(in 1963) resident of Henning, Tennessee, childhood friend of Alex Haley*

My wife cried and I remember that I wanted to cry, myself. I had feelings that, to this day, I cannot find the words to describe. I was hurt. I felt like I had been backed into a corner, and I felt anger at whoever or whatever had killed this man....We listened to the news on the car radio. We noticed people out on the streets and sidewalks, and in yards —gathered in groups and talking. It looked very unusual, but we knew what the people were talking about.

MARY TYLER MOORE, *actress*

MTM

August 14, 1980

Dear Mrs. Hansen,

I was in Sacramento filming the pilot "Slatterys People."
At that time on Friday three other actors and myself were
in an upper office of the assembly relaxing and waiting
to be used while other scenes were being shot on the floor
of the assembly. An assistant wardrobe man came into the
room and asked one actor if he could fit a suit on him.
While he was doing that, we continued to shoot the breeze.
After 20 minutes of this, as he put pins here and there,
the wardrobe man remarked, "isn't it terrible about the
president"? We said "What are you talking about?" He replie
"He's been shot" I wanted to kill him for treating it so
lightly, for treating it so inconsequentially. We raced to
the floor of the assembly and continued to receive the
news of the tragedy as it came it.

The Bishop of New York
The Rt. Rev. Paul Moore Jr.
1047 Amsterdam Avenue New York N.Y. 10025 (212) 678-6953

May 29, 1980

Mrs. Jodie Elliott Hansen
Box 1031
Union City, Tennessee 38261

Dear Mrs. Hansen:

What an interesting idea for your book!

I was sick in bed with the flu in Indianapolis, Indiana when
I heard of the President's death. My wife called from downstairs where she was in the kitchen - first that he was shot
and then a few minutes later that he had died. We switched
on the television in my bedroom and watched aghast as the
events unfolded. I remember being particularly upset that
I couldn't be at my church - Christ Church Cathedral in
Indianapolis, the following Sunday to share in the grief
that all our people felt.

I'd known Jack Kennedy personally and had only recently
visited him for a few minutes in the White House. People my
age felt of him as the first President who represented our
generation, had been through our experiences (I also was
wounded in the Pacific), and expressed our ideals. It was as
if our generation's one chance to be in a leadership position
in our nation was snatched from us.

I remember several years before when Jack Kennedy came to dinner
at our house in Florida. He sat next to my mother and during
the conversation Mother told me she turned to him and said,
"Young man, I think you're going to go a long way." That was
even before he was in Congress. He had that quality about him.

I still cannot read about it or hear about it without having a
deep pang of grief. It was like losing a brother or like re-
membering the war.

Good luck to you with your project.

Sincerely,

Bishop of New York

PM:tp

28 July 1982

Mrs.Jodie Elliott Hansen
Box 1031
Union City, Tennessee 38261

Dear Mrs. Hansen:

In response to your request that I inform you as to
what I was doing when I first heard the news of the
assassination of President John Kennedy, my account is
as follows:

At that time I was living in Yokosuka, Japan with
my family as Commander of the Seventh Fleet based in the
Western Pacific. Due to the difference in time of seven
hours, the actual news reached Japan early in the morning
and was immediately broadcast over many radios. It so
happened that my young son, Richard, was up very early
to participate in a visit to Mount Fuji by his Boy Scout
Troop. While dressing he was listening to the radio and,
of course, heard the unhappy news. He immediately informed me and at that moment my telephone began to ring
with calls from my flagship, USS PROVIDENCE, the American
Embassy in Tokyo, and the Chief of Naval Operations in
Washington, D.C. Of interest is the fact that the Japanese
conducted a ceremony in one of the larger churches in
Tokyo which even went so far as to include a coffin displayed behind the pulpit draped with an American flag.
The church was filled to overflowing and in addition
several thousand Japanese gathered outside the church to
pay their final respects to President Kennedy.

Sincerely,

Thomas H. Moorer
Admiral, U.S. Navy (Ret.)

MORT H. MOSELEY *(in 1963) family medicine physician in Eddyville, Kentucky*

The quail hunting season had opened and though it was somewhat warm I decided to try. The old dog wasn't in any better shape than I, so we struck out on Don Oliver's place not far from town. About mid-morning he pointed to a covey of the old-time big Bob Whites. As the covey rose I downed two birds, first two shots. The dog retrieved perfectly. Weather was getting too warm so decided to return home because scenting conditions were poor. Got home just before 12 o'clock noon. Wasn't seeing any patients that day so just came through my waiting room where there happened to be a TV. My wife called my attention to the tragic news out of Dallas. It was so terrible I didn't want to believe it. Nothing to do but just sit there and listen and reflect on the sad state of affairs. Did not hunt any more that Fall. This is a rare thing for any bird hunter to do—pass up quail shooting. Even my old dog seemed to sense that something had gone bad wrong. It had.

DANIEL P. MOYNIHAN
NEW YORK

United States Senate
WASHINGTON, D.C. 20510

June 28, 1980

Dear Mrs. Hansen:

Thank you so much for your thoughtful inquiry.

Although I did not know President Kennedy very well personally, I felt somehow as though I had lost a member of my own family. His assassination was the final step in my political maturation process; after the President's death, I felt that I would never be young again.

I remember very well where I was when we heard the terrible news. I was at a private home in Georgetown discussing the renovation of Pennsylvania Avenue when the news came over the radio.

Bill Walton, Charles Horsky and I grabbed a taxi to rush for the White House. When we arrived there, Ted Sorenson ran in shrieking, "It's over, he's dead."

Ironically, the White House maintenance staff had begun to change the carpeting in the Oval Office during the President's trip to Dallas so all the President's furniture was piled in the hall, including his prized rocking chair, as if someone knew that a new President would be moving in.

I hope this material will be of help.

Sincerely,

Daniel Patrick Moynihan

Mrs. Dodie Elliot Hansen
Box 1031
Union City, Tennessee 38261

KIKI SKAGEN MUNSHI *(in 1963) college student, later served many years in the U.S. Foreign Service*

I was working in the garden of one of the college professors that afternoon. Raking leaves, pulling weeds, and trimming the grass in the autumn sun, I wondered at one point why the church bells were ringing at an odd hour, then lost myself in the work again....I knew (later) why the church bells had tolled. I knew only then that they were tolling, not ringing, and I felt they were tolling for us....Looking back on it, the day was, personally, the end of an era. It marked for me, as it did for so many others, the beginning of a downhill slide in belief and commitment to the kind of things we felt Kennedy stood for. That is very much a personal perception, though, and I doubt that I see the assassination in the same light if I approach it as a historian. Times and tempers change, it is true, but there is a continuity of violence and violent reaction in this country that is almost a national characteristic. There is also a continuity in many other areas that "traumatic" events change very slightly—witness our policy toward Indochina/Vietnam. I am not sure now that our history would have been much different had the assassination not occurred.

MARGARET MURDOCK, *campanile player*

7/10/80

On the incredibly tragic day of the Kennedy assassination I was working in the office of the Women's Faculty Club on the University of California (Berkeley) campus. My office companion and I were "struck dumb" and flabbergasted, with nothing to say in our state of shock, but our office telephone never stopped ringing and at last we left it off the hook in desperation. Fortunately for me, it was not a day when I was scheduled to play the bells in the Campanile for by Pacific time the word reached us about eleven thirty in the morning. *and I often played at noon* One of my first experiences as a bell ringer in 1923 was tolling a bell for an hour as the funeral train bearing President Harding's body rolled its way from the Oakland mole toward Washington started its journey.

Happier memories of earlier presidents was in shaking hands with President Taft in 1915 when he came to the Panama Pacific Exposition, and watching a parade with President McKinley in the late nineties. I had played bells for President Kennedy when he spoke at a campus ceremony and also participated in United Nations ceremonies in our Greek Theater with national anthems from the delegates' nations. We had also joyously celebrated the armistice. Bells can express many emotions.

Margaret Murdock

GUNNAR MYRDAL, *economist, Nobel Laureate*

 INSTITUTE FOR INTERNATIONAL ECONOMIC STUDIES

Vaesterlanggatan 31
S-111 29   STOCKHOLM

. 13 August 1980

Mrs. Jodie Elliott Hansen
Box 1031
UNION CITY, Tennessee 38261
U S A

Dear Mrs. Hansen,

Alva and I had two friends from the deplomatic corps as guests
for dinner when the message came. I wrote an article for the
periodical Vi in Sweden.

Patrick Moynihan, who at that time was working in the Labor
Department in Washington, told me once that he was informed
about Kennedy's murder when he came to the White House on some
business mission. He was shocked and walked around aimlessly
in the White House and finally found himself in the Oval Room.
Kennedy had left two things on his table: a vase with one red
rose and my little book Challenge to Affluence. Kennedy had
prepared Johnson's unconditional war against poverty which
Johnson then took up.

With kind regards,

Cordially yours,

Gunnar Myrdal

NEAL & HARWELL

8TH FLOOR, THIRD NATIONAL BANK BUILDING

NASHVILLE, TENNESSEE 37219

(615) 244-1713

December 9, 1981

JAMES F. NEAL
AUBREY B. HARWELL, JR.
JON D. ROSS
JAMES V. DORAMUS
JAMES F. SANDERS
THOMAS H. DUNDON
ROBERT L. SULLIVAN
RONALD G. HARRIS
ALBERT F. MOORE

MITCHELL ROGOVIN
OF COUNSEL
(NOT ADMITTED IN TENNESSEE)

Mrs. Jodie Elliott Hansen
Box 1031
Union City, TN 38261

Dear Jodie:

I remember very vividly the assassination of President Kennedy, my location at the time, my actions and my emotions.

First, let me say that my wife and I were invited to attend the last White House reception held by President Kennedy before he left on his trip to Texas. My wife attended, but I was unable to because I was in Nashville, Tennessee preparing for the second Hoffa trial. (This trial actually took place starting in January of 1964, in Chattanooga and ended in March of the same year, with the first conviction ever of Jimmy Hoffa.) I was in the library of the United States Attorney's Office when my secretary came back and told me that President Kennedy had been shot and his condition was unknown. I immediately went down to the office of my friend, John Seigenthaler, who is now Publisher of The Nashville Tennessean and was at that time the Editor. John and I had worked in the Kennedy Administration and both were acquaintances of the President and very good friends of his brother, Robert Kennedy.

We spent the rest of the day in Mr. Seigenthaler's office listening to the news accounts. When it became clear that President Kennedy was dead or dying, I immediately caught a plane back to Washington, D.C. I, of course, was devastated. I vividly remember being on the plane and two people were discussing rather ordinary events of the world and of their private lives as if nothing had happened. Somehow this just overwhelmed me, and I accosted these gentlemen with the fact that President Kennedy had been killed and they were going along discussing day to day affairs. I think I was so incensed, I could have

Mrs. Jodie Elliott Hansen
Page 2
December 9, 1981

shot them both.

Upon returning to Washington, I got with other friends
and supporters of the Kennedy Administration and spent the
rest of the weekend involved in the funeral and the aftermath
of the Kennedy assassination.

I think for many of us, we died a little that tragic
weekend. I know that my own ambition and confident view of
life and of my own future abated considerably following that
terrible event. No longer, and never since, have I thought
it advisable or relevant to make long-range plans. Moreover,
no longer did I view the world as capable of being conquered
nor did I view myself as being able to control even my own
destiny much less making a substantial and lasting contribution
to society. In short, I think my view of the world, myself,
and my relationship to the world changed irrevocably on that
weekend.

In view of the above, you can imagine the added effect
many of us felt in 1968 when Bob Kennedy, along with Martin
Luther King, was assassinated.

I hope this accounting contributes to your effort.

Sincerely,

James F. Neal

JIMMY "BOATS" NEWBERRY *(in 1963) manufacturing executive in Memphis, Tennessee; since 1967, president and director of P.T. Boats, Inc., a nonprofit organization established to preserve the history of Patrol Torpedo Boats*

My memories of JFK go back to 1943 when we were in the South Pacific during the war. Kennedy was the commander or skipper of PT-109 when they were attacked by the Japanese, and he earned a citation for valor for saving the lives of several of his crewmen. I was the Chief Boatswain on the commanding officer's boat—the PT-157, which was the boat that picked up the crew of PT-109 after their mishap.

When we arrived the coastwatcher had already picked up JFK in a dugout, covering him with brush and palm leaves and had taken him back to Rendova Base.

JFK was well liked and mixed well with others. Everyone knew his father was the ambassador to Great Britain and I feel certain that he most likely got special favors from the higher-ups, but the other crewmen did not treat him any differently because of his family's wealth and his father's prestige.

He was a nice young man, a pleasant and personable skinny young man. He was bright and intelligent, but not exceptionally so. I never once speculated or even entertained the thought that he would ever be President of the United States. I doubt that Jack himself, at that time, had such lofty ideas or ever expected to someday be in the White House.

Jack Kennedy was a fairly good P.T. boat skipper and was heroic in the way he rescued the 9–10 crew members, but he should have been court-martialed for losing the boat in the first place. Jack Kennedy tore down more docks than anyone in the South Pacific. He acted like he was in a motorboat. Jack's talents and expertise were in sailing and not in docking P.T. Boats.

The two of us would frequently have discussions about the Civil War— the issues, the different battles, etc. Being a native of Arkansas, I consider myself a Rebel and a Conservative. JFK was a Yankee, a Bostonian, and a Liberal. To say we had opposing views is putting it mildly. Even though JFK was wrong on many issues, he was well-read and well-informed on the Civil War.

I voted for Kennedy in the 1960 election and admit that his being a P.T. Boat veteran had something to do with it. Even though I did not agree with some of his policies, I thought he was sincere and would give the job his all. I wrote to him several times, when I didn't agree with him on specific issues, especially the Bay of Pigs and the civil rights issues. The President always answered my letters, and I knew by the tone of them that JFK had personally dictated them. I honestly can't remember where I was when I first heard the news of the assassination. I do remember that weekend and feeling absolutely terrible. I'm not a TV watcher but most of the weekend I stayed with the television set and immediately sent a letter of condolence to the Kennedy family.

WILLIAM CARL NOLAN *(in 1963) college professor at Southern Arkansas University*

Not everyone in the community was equally saddened by the news of his death or impressed about the possible consequences that might follow. There were reports that some school children were somewhat jubilant over the news. I was greatly disappointed when the school system in which my own children were registered refused to dismiss school for the funeral which was televised. I had them stay home for that event, even though the school charged them with an unexcused absence. Few of us today recall the mixed emotions that were displayed during that turbulent period. For most of us it was a very sad occasion. But for a few, the President's death seemed to promise an end to the segregation controversy that gripped the community. Because of these mixed feelings, I believe many tragic events could have followed in clashes between these groups. We owe a great deal to the masterful and inspired manner in which Lyndon Johnson assumed the office of President and political leadership of the nation at that critical moment.

DR. ALTON OCHSNER, *surgeon, pioneered "war on smoking"*

OCHSNER CLINIC
1514 JEFFERSON HIGHWAY
NEW ORLEANS, LA. 70121
CABLE ADDRESS: OCHSCLINIC

DEPARTMENT OF GENERAL SURGERY

ROBERT M. ARENSMAN, M.D.
JOHN B. BLALOCK, M.D.
JOHN C. BOWEN, M.D.
PAUL T. DECAMP, M.D.
ROBERT C. LYNCH, M.D.
JOSEPH F. MABEY, M.D.
WILLIAM M. P. McKINNON, M.D.
NOEL L. MILLS, M.D.
ALTON OCHSNER, M.D.
JOHN L. OCHSNER, M.D.

TELEPHONE: 838-4000
AREA CODE: 504

May 14, 1981

Mrs. Jodie Elliott Hansen
Box 1031
Union City, TN 38261

Dear Mrs. Hansen:

Thank you for your letter of April 27. I was in Sydney, Australia
when President John Kennedy was shot. I was President of the Pan-
Pacific Surgical Society, which meets in Hawaii, and we took a post-
convention trip to the Asian countries. At five o'clock in the morning I was called by the Press because they knew there was a group of
Americans there to tell us that our President had been shot. It was
unbelievable. When I learned that Oswald had done it, I could understand it because I have been head of an organization which has been
fighting communism for a number of years and we had interviewed Owwald
and showed that he was a Marxist. Still, it was just unbelievable
that a person would do that.

It is tragic that there is a group of people out to destroy the western
type of civilization, and we are going to have these terrorists for a
long time, although I think they can be controlled if more people would
be aware of it and take action about it.

Thanking you for your letter and with kind regards, I am

Yours very sincerely,

Alton Ochsner, M. D.

AO:frb

THOMAS P. O'NEILL, *U.S. Representative from Massachusetts, Speaker of the House*

The Speaker's Rooms
U. S. House of Representatives
Washington, D. C. 20515

January 30, 1980

Mrs. Jodie Elliott Hansen
Box 1031
Union City, Tennessee 38261

Dear Mrs. Hansen:

The day Jack Kennedy was shot, I was in my Boston office seeing constituents when my secretary interrupted us to tell us of a report that the Presdient had been shot.

She said she couldn't believe it, so I called the Boston Globe. The switchboard recognized me and said, "Is that you, Mr. O'Neill? It's true, he's been shot," and burst out crying.

The news shook me because not only had the United States and the world lost a great leader, but I had lost a dear friend. The tears rolled down my cheeks and I felt a weakness in my heart.

Sincerely,

Thomas P. O'Neill, Jr.
The Speaker

H/rh

EUGENE ORMANDY, *classical conductor and violinist*

The Philadelphia Orchestra Association

EUGENE ORMANDY, MUSIC DIRECTOR

OFFICE OF THE MUSIC DIRECTOR

1420 LOCUST STREET, PHILADELPHIA, PA. 19102
TELEPHONE: (215) 893-1900 CABLE ADDRESS "PHILAORCH"

March 11, 1979

Mrs. Jodie Elliott Hansen
Box 1031
Union City, Tennessee 38261

Dear Mrs. Hansen:

I vividly recall the circumstances surrounding the tragic
news of the assassination of President John F. Kennedy.

I was conducting the Philadelphia Orchestra in the Friday
afternoon concert and we had just started the "Wedding March"
from Mendelssohn's "A Midsummer Night's Dream" when someone
off stage snapped his fingers beckoning me to stop playing.
I knew that something had happened so I walked off the stage
to get the news from our Manager, Mr. Sokoloff,' that the President
had been shot in Dallas, but we had no further news. I was
asked to stay back stage to await more information and almost
immediately we heard that the President was dead. Naturally,
I asked the Manager to make an announcement from the stage and
I decided not to continue the concert. About an hour later I
had a call from one of the Executives of CBS in New York
asking me if I could perfrom the Brahms German Requiem the
following afternoon. We assembled the cast and the Rutgers
University Choir for an emergency rehearsal with the Columbia
Broadcasting group and in the afternoon we gave a performance
so moving that I don't think there were many dry eyes at the
end of the performance. It is a day I shall never forget.

Sincerely yours,

Eugene Ormandy

JEROLD D. OTTLEY, *music director, Mormon Tabernacle Choir*

THE SALT LAKE
MORMON TABERNACLE CHOIR
50 EAST NORTH TEMPLE STREET   THE CHURCH OF JESUS CHRIST OF LATTER-DAY SAINTS   TELEPHONE
SALT LAKE CITY, UTAH 84150   (801) 531-3221

August 20, 1981

Mrs. Jodie Elliott Hansen
Box 1031
Union City, Tennessee 38261

Dear Mrs. Hansen,

        The news that President John F. Kennedy had been shot came to my ears
first as a rumor. I was a teacher of choral music in a Salt Lake City suburban high school. A class was gathering after the lunch hour and I observed
some girls in tears as they were discussing the news reports of the shooting.
I immediately sent a class representative to the school office to find out
if this report was bonafide. Before the report was confirmed, the school
principal interrupted classes by intercom to announce that President Kennedy
was dead.

        My class was an all-girl, sophomore (10th grade) chorus with mixed
social backgrounds. Some were earnestly interested in music, while others were
sent to the class by school counselors because of their trouble-making attitudes
in other areas of the school. As a result of this mixture, the reaction to the
announcement was a combination of horror, disbelief, and defensiveness. The
more serious girls were sobered and many wept. The less socially secure girls
tried to cover their shock by denigrating those who showed their emotions openly.
One or two hard core types actually joked aloud, but with half-hearted embarrass-
ment. We listened for a few moments to the continuing news reports and then as
the intercom fell silent, so did the classroom. We had been instructed that
school would recess early, so for a few moments we marked time without comment.
Then an unusual and exciting thing happened. One of the girls began singing
softly "America, The Beautiful". Others hesitantly joined until the entire
class was singing. Again, there was a short silence. A particularly thoughtful
girl asked if it would be alright if we prayed. When I found no objection from
the others in the class, she enunciated a thoughtful and moving prayer which
included concern for those who had perpetrated the assassination. A few moments
later, school was dismissed and we rushed to our homes to follow the media coverage of the succeeding events.

Mrs. Jodie Elliott Hansen

Page Two

I was, at that time, a relatively new singing member of the Mormon Tabernacle Choir and on Sunday, November 24th participated with the Choir in an hour long nationwide TV broadcast and tribute to the assassinated President.

On a personal basis, these few days were some of the most important of my life. I came to grips personally with the event and with what it meant to our nation. More importantly, it helped to establish in my mind, the role of the President regardless of the individual who holds the office. Since that time, I have had the opportunity of performing with the Tabernacle Choir for four Presidents, two as a singer, and two as the conductor of the Choir.

Best wishes in your project.

Sincerely,

Jerold D. Ottley

JDO/as

GEORGE S. PATTON, III, *U.S. Army General*

Major General George Smith Patton
United States Army, Retired
650 Asbury Street
South Hamilton, Massachusetts 01982
(617) 468-4533

1 December 1980

Mrs. Jodie E. Hansen
Box 1031
Union City, Tennessee   38261

Dear Mrs. Hansen:

Thanks for your letter. I will have difficulty
expressing myself with reference to your book which
I feel is a worthwhile effort.

I was in the chapel at Fort Hood, Texas when this
occurred. At the time of the assassination, I was
commanding the 2nd Medium Tank Battalion, 81st Armor,
1st Armored Division, Fort Hood, Texas. We were under-
going a National Day of Prayer, which is something
that the Army does once a year and soldiers of all
faiths and color are encouraged very strongly to go
to church on that day. There is no formal training on
that day. At any rate, I was in the service when we
received word through the chaplain that President
Kennedy had been injured seriously in an assassination
attempt. Of course, prayers were arranged in his behalf
and within fifteen or twenty minutes, we received word
that he had expired. We then all got up and sang, as
I recall, "Onward Christian Soldiers," had another
prayer and left.

Upon leaving the chapel, we were then alerted that we
were to remain in our quarters or in our barracks for
the next twenty-four hours in the event of some kind
of a disturbance in the Dallas area. Of course, there
was no disturbance and everything continued as normal
the next morning. That is how I remember my experiences
on the day of the assassination of President John F.
Kennedy. I hope this has been of some help to you and
I send you my best regards.

Faithfully,

George S. Patton
Major General
US Army, Retired

GSP:nks

NBC News   A Division of   Thirty Rockefeller Plaza
                National Broadcasting Company, Inc.   New York, N.Y. 10020   212-664-2621

                Jane Pauley
                TODAY

March 31, 1980

Mrs. Jodie Elliott Hansen
Box 1031
Union City, Tenn. 38261

Dear Mrs. Hansen,

I think you have a fine idea and look forward to
seeing the finished product.

My story, however, is not worthy of your book.
I was just a thirteen year old kid in a school
cafeteria. I was too young to give you the kind
of recollections that should be put in
a historical account.

But, best of luck.

Sincerely,

Jane Pauley

JP:as

Minnie Pearl

I was in Jackson,
Miss. when I heard
the news of the
death of President
Kennedy. It seemed
completely unreal.
I had written a
little christmas
book and was
autographing the
book in the book
dept of a store
when a whitefaced
young man dashed
up and yelled,
"President Kennedy
has been shot!"
we all just froze
where we were.

Minnie Pearl

There was a TV set nearby and we all gathered around it in shocked, numb fascination. I felt as I did when Pearl Harbor was bombed. My world was threatened. I wanted to go back to my childhood and have Mama tell me everything was going to be all right again.

CARL PERKINS *(in 1963) rockabilly musician*

My hit record, "Blue Swede Shoes," was big, back in the jitterbug days of the late '50s and early '60s and I believe it was during the Kennedy term that this record was added to the collection in the White House. I feel that JFK was the type of man who would have liked this song. I feel that he would have appreciated the color and humor of it. I even feel that at some time, back in those days, that he most likely shook a leg to it. . . . I never thought I would be a witness to an assassination of the leader of the greatest nation on earth, and then not only this assassination, but all the events that followed. Lee Harvey Oswald being shot by Jack Ruby; Robert Kennedy's and the Black leader, Martin Luther King's deaths. I believe America took a turn when that bullet was fired, when that trigger was pulled in Dallas. America made a drastic turn. There was a feeling like the days of the Old West had come back to America, and it was going to be the gun again. It was such an uneasy feeling, and still today, it seems like way down deep something is getting ready to boil.

MARLIN R. PERKINS, *zoologist, television host,* Mutual of Omaha's
Wild Kingdom

R. MARLIN PERKINS
52 ABERDEEN PLACE
SAINT LOUIS, MISSOURI 63105

Sept. 1, 1983

Dear Mrs Hansen:

When President John Kennedy was
assassinated I was in a restaurant not far from the
St. Louis Zoo when the news came in by radio.
My first reaction was "how could this happen?",
then anger that someone had killed <u>my</u> president,
then a debilating feeling of sadness and loss.
After all the publicity in the press and media I still
find it difficult to understand how such a thing could
happen in the United States of America.

Sincerely,

Marlin Perkins

LAURENCE J. PETER, *author*, The Peter Principle

2332 Via Anacapa,
Palos Verdes Est., Ca. 90274.
October 23, 1982

Dear Mrs. Hansen:

I was at Dawson School in Vancouver, B.C. counseling a boy
who was having learning problems when a teacher, Don
Cross, who had been listening to the radio came into
my office and told me that President Kennedy had been
shot. Only details of the motorcade, the time, and the
place were available. His wounds were reported to be
of a serious nature. I tried to return to my work but was
unable to concentrate on the boy's problem so sent him
back to his classroom. I went to the faculty room and
shortly heared, over the radio, that the president had
died. Although I was not an American I did not think
that my outrage or sense of loss could have been greater.
Like so many, the world over, I had placed my hopes for
a better future in the leadership of John F. Kennedy.

Laurence J. Peter
Author; The Peter Principle.

Roberta Peters

April 21, 1982

Mrs. Jodie Elliott Hansen
Box 1031
Union City, Tenn. 38261

Dear Mrs. Hansen:

Thank you very much for your letter of April 7th.
I am replying to your request of my memories of the day
that President Kennedy was assassinated:

I had been giving a series of concerts in the
Northwestern part of the U.S. Seattle and
Tacoma were the last two. The morning after
the concert in Tacoma, I was flying to Los Angeles
to meet my husband who was coming from New York
for a much needed vacation. While on the plane
that morning, the captain had announced that the
President had been shot. The airplane was in
an uproar, but we were still hopeful that he
might still recover and that it would not be
fatal. When the plane landed in Los Angeles,
my husband was at the ramp and from the expression
on his face, I could tell the news was bad. When
we got into the airport lounge, people were crying
and we sat with them dazed. We did go on to
Palm Springs for our vacation, but stayed in the
room the whole time glued to the television and
witnessed the funeral and the horrible events
following the funeral, namely Mr. Ruby shooting
Mr. Oswald.

All best wishes for your book and I would appreciate
having a copy when it comes out.

Sincerely,

Roberta Peters.

October 9th

Dear Mrs. Hansen,

I have just returned from Europe to
find your letter about my memory of
the day of the assassination.

I shall await with interest your
story.

Best wishes to you,

Sincerely,

Elly M. Peterson

I remember the day of Pres. Kennedy's assassination clearly

I was attending a Republican Regional Meeting in St. Louis
Missouri. At that time I had just gone with the National
Committee as Executive Director of the Womens Division and
it was my first national meeting.

About 10 people had arrived in St. Louis the day before
the meeting opened to plan the procedures...and that morning the lobby had been decorated with banners and signs
and three rocking chairs - one for each of the Kennedy
brothers. The President was to be the target of the
meeting.

With the plans underway and my superior, Clare Williams
Shank - vice Chairman of the National Committee - not
yet arrived, I seized the time to go to the beauty parlor
and was under the dryer when the hairdresser lifted the
hood and said, "Kennedy has been shot". Like a bolt, I
was out of my chair and out the door headed for our
headquarters office.

The situation there was tense. The National Chairman was
enroute from Washington - but the group moved into action
and the lobby was stripped quickly of signs AND chairs.
A press conference was set up for Chairman Miller and
Mrs. Shank and a lookout was posted in the lobby as they
probably would not know what had happened.

The office was buzzing but quietly - whispered conversations: many thought the conservatives had shot him, some
thought it was because he was in Texas and I remember Sen.
Tower on the telephone to Washington, frantic for the safety
of his family. Staff members appeared to be too stunned to
do more than what they were exactly directed to do.

Within an hour, the Chairman arrived, held his press confer
ence - and the Conference was over before it began. I drove
out to Vandalia, Illinois to the home of a friend for over-
night and saw Oswald killed on the TV - then flew back to
Washington where two women from my office met me and drove
me to the Capitol.

The streets of Washington were NEVER as they were that night;
so quiet they were eerie. Long lines were heading towards
the Capitol - four deep - shuffle, shuffle quietly...now and
then a cough - now and then a baby would cry out only to be
quieted at once - shuffle, shuffle...It was a mood that
lasted through the Capitol and memorial services.

G EORGE H. P OLLOCK, *director, Institute for Psychoanalysis*

The
Institute
For
Psychoanalysis

180 N. MICHIGAN AVENUE

CHICAGO

ILLINOIS 60601

PHONE 726/6300

February 15, 1980

Mrs. Jodie Elliott Hansen
Box 1031
Union City, TN 38261

Dear Mrs. Hansen,

Thank you for your letter of January 29 inviting me
to comment on my reactions at the time of the assassination of the late President John F. Kennedy for
inclusion in your book.

At the time, I was on a visit to Dublin and recall
that I was on my way to the Abby Theater. As I left
the Gresham Hotel and was walking to the theater,
several people approached me and spoke to me about
the tragedy. I had not yet heard of it and was, of
course, initially shocked and filled with disbelief,
and then, felt a sense of dispair.

The response of the Dubliners ranged from out-right
anger voiced by "why did you do this to our Jack" to
compassion expressed by "I am very sorry that the U.S.
has lost a great man." I kept thinking about the
tragedy throughout the performance, and when I left
the theater later, I learned that President Kennedy
was, in fact, dead. I could not sleep that night,
thinking about how his parents, wife, children and
siblings must have felt. The family had had much
tragedy as well as triumphs, and no one imagined that
there would be even more tragedy in the wings.

My own research in the mourning-bereavement process
helped me greatly. I was able to understand why many
people who did not know the president personally acted
as if they had had a personal loss -- they did, sym-
bolically. And, of course, the entire world grieved
for him.

Several of my friends called me in Dublin, and I
called my family in Chicago to share some of my very
sad feelings with them. The response to the death
of President Kennedy was similar to the response I
had to the death of President Roosevelt. It is true
that the two were not comparable in that President
Roosevelt was older and was ill, but still, his
death was unexpected and he had been a president
during trying circumstances. The death of President
Kennedy and the ambience that he had brought seemed
to be a greater tragedy -- he was a younger man and
had small children. When I spoke of the assassination
with my London friends, after visiting Dublin, my
colleagues there shared with me their responses to
the death of King George VI which were similar, and
subsequently I remember reading and seeing the same
responses to the death of President Nasser in Egypt.

I hope that this is of some interest to you, and I
look forward to reading the book. Would you please
send any further correspondence to my office address
rather than to the University and this will avoid
any delays.

With best wishes,

George H. Pollock, M.D.
Director

Melodie E. Hansen
Box 1031
Union City,
Tennessee 38261

Dear Mrs Hansen
I was filming in London, a
picture called "The Masque of The Red
Death". I stopped by the U.S Embassy
to sign a book of Condolences then
drove to the Studio. Being the only
U.S. Citizen on The film I was asked to
say a few words to the grief stricken
English Cast + Crew — It was difficult
to say The least — all Britain was at
half mast for That Great man
Sincerely Vincent Price

GEORGE PSYCHAS *(in 1963) working at a teacher training college in Tanzania with the organization Teachers for East Africa*

(After hearing the news) I walked about a quarter of a mile down a dirt road to the school and will never forget seeing the 25–30 people assembled there to pay their respects and condolences to me because I was an American, and our country's leader had been shot. I was quite touched by this gesture, as I was unaware that the laborers (subordinate staff as they were called by the British) even knew or cared about President Kennedy. I later learned that indeed they did, and many of them had pictures of him, and that their leader, President Julius Nyerere, considered himself to be a good friend of JFK's. By the time I had finished shaking hands with each one of them, I was emotionally overcome. There was a genuine sadness about them—a shrugging of the shoulders, a kind of whine in their voices. This was their way of expressing this deep emotion they felt.

President Nyerere had declared a national day of mourning. As a matter of fact, I believe it was more than one day. I was free to leave the school since it was closed and I had this urgent need to be with other Americans. I drove to a village about 3 miles away. When I arrived, there were other Americans there including Peace Corps people who had apparently felt this same need. They were coming in from all over the bush. We had no telephones and of course, no televisions. Our communications system consisted

(continued)

of the bush grapevine or bush telephone, as we called it. News of everything traveled very rapidly by word of mouth. Shortwave radios were our means of official news of this horrible thing that had occurred in America. We all gathered around the radio to catch whatever bits of information we could from the BBC, Voice of America, Voice of Cairo, etc. Later on that day I went into town and was surprised to find they had ceased to do business. The town had literally closed up and the people were just sort of milling around in the streets.

Another interesting observation concerning how the Africans felt about JFK is reflected in the "Kennedy posho." I would travel from village to village as part of my work and we would distribute this maize to the villages, particularly to those who had famines at various times. This maize was in 50-pound sacks and each sack would have a picture of a shield on it with the American flag on the shield and a black hand clasping a white hand. The people called this maize "Kennedy posho." I've just returned from spending two more years there and I saw this maize and that shield—and I do not recall hearing anyone call it "Carter posho." It might be Swahili slang, but the word means: something extra—a supplement—a bonus or extra gift, sort of an unofficial fringe benefit. In this case, it was something extra from President Kennedy.

Even though it wasn't true, the people there thought we were working for President Kennedy. We were not directly involved with the Peace Corps but I think it's fair to say that JFK created an attitude about government *and government service that did not exist before he was in office and that he drew large numbers of young people into government. It's clear to me that I joined this government project to serve and to be part of this spirit during those times. Many, many times after the assassination, I had the feeling that someone should be told about the reactions of these people.*

There was something about the man and the times that caused the people to behave as they did. What I hope is captured by the books and the media is this feeling that our nation had—and the personal involvement so many of us experienced in our attempts to make the world a better one. If JFK had lived and served another term, perhaps the record would be much different than it is, but at that time, it was the spirit that was such a part of the whole world. I got caught up in it—not in Kennedy himself—but in the inspiration of his dreams, I suppose. Even though I was a bachelor at the time I had many, many reasons to stay here (in America) but suddenly one day I decided to get on the bandwagon, so to speak, and I signed up to go to Africa. I suppose it was the times and my age. I believe this spirit created by JFK continued for about a year or so until LBJ was elected in '64 and as the war situation became more complex, the so-called cynicism set in.

DENNIS RALSTON, *professional tennis player*

March 25, 1981

Mrs. Jodie Elliott Hansen
Box 1031
Union City, Tennessee 38261

Dear Mrs. Hansen:

I was in Australia with the U.S.A. Davis Cup Team when
I heard about President Kennedy's death.

We were in Adeliade where we were participating in a
tournament prior to our final Davis Cup match with Australia.

I heard the news early in the morning as I was getting
up to have breakfast. At first I did not believe it but
the reports continued and I knew something had happened.

I remember that I was stunned and felt awful. I was
scheduled that day to play in the finals of the tournament
but wanted to default and not play.

Our ambassador to Australia, Bill Battle, talked to
me and convinced me to play in the finals. He had been
a close friend of President Kennedy's and stressed that I
should represent America at this time and that President
Kennedy would have wanted me to play.

I hope this is what you need.

Sincerely,

Dennis Ralston

Dennis Ralston

DR/mg

James Earl Ray, *convicted assassin of Martin Luther King, Jr.*

4/20/81

Dear Mrs. Hansen: James E. Ray

I was in prison at the time JFK was assaulted consequently things (news items)
are second hand by the time they arrive. For legal reasons I can't comment on
controversial legal cases, although unlike thoes responsible for investigating the
JFK case, including the dominant press, my reaction wasn't to think how I could
contain the investigation.

Sincerely:

James E. Ray

THE WHITE HOUSE

July 20, 1982

Dear Mrs. Hansen:

The following is my reaction to the news
of the assassination of President John
Kennedy:

I was in the car driving to an appointment and heard the news on the radio. I
couldn't believe what I heard. I pulled
over to the side of the road, stayed there
for a long while and cried. It seemed
unbelievable that something like that
could happen in our country.

Sincerely,

Nancy Reagan

Mrs. Jodie Elliott Hansen
Box 1031
Union City
Tennessee 38261

Vɪʟᴍᴀ Rᴏʙᴀɪɴᴀ *(in 1963) residing in New Orleans, left Cuba in 1961*

We, and all of our Cuban friends, were quite emotional about JFK's death. We were impressed and somewhat in awe of the dignified funeral ceremony and the composure of the Kennedy family, especially his wife. Their calmness was unbelievable and such a contrast to the emotional manner our people express grief. . . . At the time of the assassination my feelings for President Kennedy were (and are) mixed. I was very sad that he was killed but I still had the hurt and anger from the Bay of Pigs incident and yet I admired him for the stand he took during the Cuban Missile Crisis. Being objective and thinking in terms of American politics, his actions or betrayal of my people might have been necessary or unavoidable at the time, but if he had taken a stand then it might have stopped Castro's attempts to spread Communism in South American countries and other underdeveloped countries.

The President's Advisory Committee for Women

200 Constitution Avenue, N.W., Washington, D.C. 20210
Room N-3437 (202) 523-6707

December 4, 1979

HONORARY CHAIR:
Judy Carter

CHAIR:
Lynda Johnson Robb

VICE CHAIRS:
Marjorie Bell Chambers
Elizabeth Koontz

MEMBERS:

Owanah Anderson
Unita Blackwell
Erma Bombeck
Jack T. Conway
Miriam I. Cruz
Laura deHerrera
Donna E. deVarona
Gretta Dewald
Charles Guerrier
Nancy Humphries
Jeffalyn Johnson
Odessa Komer
Esther Landa
Linda J. Lee
Mary Helen Madden
Billie Nave Masters
Alice McDonald
Brenda Parker
Estelle Ramey
Ann S. Ramsay
Ann Richards
Richard Rossie
Jill L. Schropp
Tin Myaing Thein

Mrs. Jodie Elliott Hansen
Box 1031
Union City, Tennessee 38261

Dear Mrs. Hansen:

Please forgive me for not answering your very interesting letter sooner. It is a subject that is too close and I find I am unable to write about it as you wished.

For history, some time ago I wrote a very personal note privately to my children, which will be opened when they are old enough to appreciate it. I am sorry that I am unable to comply with your request.

Sincerely,

Lynda Johnson Robb
Chair

VERA ROBERTS *(in 1963) American housewife in Wollongong, Australia*

It was early in the morning (approximately 6:00 A.M.) when I heard the news of the assassination. Our milkman, when leaving the milk at the doorstep, rang the doorbell to tell us the news. He had never done this before and he seemed very upset about telling us of our American leader's death. He, along with other Australians, absolutely adored John F. Kennedy. At that time it seemed to me that all Australians very much liked all Americans, and I attribute this to General MacArthur's promotion of goodwill between the two countries. . . . I remember the telephone ringing off the wall all day long, people of Australia offering their sympathy and emotional support. The newspaper also called wanting to know my feelings and reaction to the American tragedy.

CLIFF ROBERTSON, *actor*

Mrs. Hody Elliott Hansen   April 7, 1980
Box 1031
Union City Tennessee 38261

Dear Mrs. Hansen;
    Thank you for your letter of February 19th. You
asked me for my reactions to the first news of the assi-
assination of our late President, John F. Kennedy.
Ironically, at the time, I was being interviewed on the
telephone in Pacific Palasades , California by a writer for
United Press Int.. He was asking me questions relative to
my having been selected by the President to portray his
role in "PT 109." During the interview, he stopped it and said
"hold it a minute, Cliff," - and when he returned to the
phone he said " are you sitting down?" - I replied, "yes,"
and he told me the news. We terminated the phone call and
I sat stunned on the edge of the bed. Some minutes later
the front door rang. It was my secretary, Mrs. Christel.
I opened the door and she was standing on the doorstep pale and
wane and in tears.
    The rest of the day was a dream - like montage of radio,
television broadcasts and telephone calls. I remember spacifically
driving to Hollywood and being made aware that not one automobile
horn sound could be heard anywhere. Shocked reverence seemed
to permeate. Everything and everyone decellerated. There
was a sense of "this couldn't have happened."

                              Respectively,

                              Cliff Robertson

CC/jo

THOMAS H. ROBINSON *(in 1963) federal prisoner at the U.S. Penitentiary in Atlanta, Georgia*

All appeals, motions, writs, petitions for clemency failed until friends of mine presented a Petition for Clemency to President Kennedy in the spring of 1963. President Kennedy said it was a little too early following an escape but he promised to release me if my sponsors would again present the petition to him on March 1, 1964. His untimely and tragic death was tantamount to another death sentence for me. On November 22, 1963, I was walking down the tier of the honor unit where I was housed when I heard someone say the President had been killed. I felt a constriction in my chest like a huge hand was squeezing my heart.

RALPH JACKSON ROGERS *(in 1963) graduate student at University of Mississippi (Ole Miss)*

We had missed the Meredith integration crisis and the federal troop occupation of Ole Miss but were well aware of the intense feelings of the townspeople about the series of incidents leading to the riots and bloodshed. Many at the university were considered "integrationists or worse," including Dr. J. W. Silver of the history department, who was one of the prime reasons for my attendance at the university. Feelings, then, were at least on edge or bruised when the Kennedy assassination occurred.

My children brought home the same story from school: cheers in the classroom when the assassination was announced and a general joyous atmosphere, a condition that neither of mine (thank God) felt. I was exposed to the intensity of feeling on the downtown square of Oxford at one of the drugstores in the town when I was purchasing an item about 5:00 P.M. on the 22nd. The pharmacist commented to a customer and friend that "he got what he deserved and I am damned glad the son of a bitch is dead." I was so taken aback that I forgot the better part of valor was discretion and stated that no matter how bitter a person's feeling were about JFK we had lost a president and all of us should be saddened about that. I got no response other than a stare from both men.

CESAR ROMERO, *actor*

Cesar Romero

Dec. 5, 1981

Dear Mrs. Hansen:

In answer to your request, I first heard of President Kennedy's assassination when I returned home after doing some errands in town. When I arrived home my sister met me at the door and said "President Kennedy has been assassinated in Dallas". I remember saying "Oh my God". I couldn't believe it. I think I was in a state of shock. I rushed to the television set and sat glued to it for the rest of the day. I'm a dyed in the wool Republican but I shed a tear for that young man, for his family and for our country. It also made me realize what a dangerous world we lived in.

I wish you great success with your book. Have a happy holiday season.

Sincerely,

Cesar Romero

TWX 910-595-1722

JAMES ROOSEVELT & CO.
110 NEWPORT CENTER DRIVE
SUITE 200
NEWPORT BEACH, CALIFORNIA 92660
—
(714) 640-8167

March 4, 1980

Mrs. Jodie Elliot Hansen
Box 1031
Union City, Tennessee 38261

Dear Mrs. Hansen:

In answer to your interesting letter and its enclosures, I am, of
course, happy to send you my recollections. You have certainly
collected a most interesting and varied set of reactions to a very
emtional and tragic time.

At the day of President Kennedy's assassination I was in my home,
just outside of Washington, D.C. in nearby Virginia. As a member
of Congress and as a long time friend of the Kennedy family, I had
had the opportunity to participate in some of the President's legis-
lation programs as well as to feel close to the President and his
family on a very personal basis. I remember watching television
that afternoon when the program was interrupted with the news that
the President had been shot in Dallas. Over the next few hours,
of course, the drama was played out. It was a cold winter day and
I will always feel it was sort of an unreal experience. One almost
felt it was something out of Orson Welles. As I remember, my emotions
were really divided into separate parts; one of absolute devastation
for the loss of John Kennedy and a feeling of helplessness in wanting
but not being able to help the family. Secondly, my thoughts had also
turned to the Vice President who had so unexpectedly become President.
He was so different in background and personality than the President.
I sat down and wrote the incoming President a short letter and drove
over to his house to hand deliver it.

Certainly my reaction to the event was not different than most Americans. We react rather unanimously as a nation to tragedy, crises and moments of real national fear.

I was, of course, directly in touch with my brother, Franklin, Jr., who was part of the Kennedy administration. I can best sum up, I think, the feeling of both of us as part shock and horror and particularly a deep personal grief coupled with a confused desire to do personally and officially whatever would help in getting over the period of obvious crisis.

May I wish you all good luck in your book. Please let me know when it is published as I would like to obtain a copy of it. Perhaps you will drop me a note to let me know where I can secure a copy.

Sincerely,

James Roosevelt

James Roosevelt

JR/sw

DEAN RUSK, *U.S. Secretary of State*

THE UNIVERSITY OF GEORGIA

SCHOOL OF LAW

ATHENS, GEORGIA 30601

April 16, 1979

Mrs. Jodie E. Hansen
Box 1031
Union City, Tennessee 38261

Dear Mrs. Hansen:

This is in response to your letter of March 12. Because of another commitment I was forced to leave the University of Mississippi before the entire seminar was over.

In answer to the questions you posed in your letter, there is no way in which I can adequately express my personal feelings on the day of President Kennedy's assassination. Six members of the Cabinet were on the way to Japan to attend a joint U. S.-Japanese Cabinet meeting. These meetings had been agreed to by President Kennedy and the Japanese Prime Minister. Our plane was one hour west of Hawaii when the word came through of the attack on President Kennedy. We immediately turned around, refueled in Hawaii and made a non-stop flight to WAshington. Beyond the shock and sorrow of that terrible tragedy, we all realized that we had to keep the public business going and help bring our country through one of its most difficult moments.

Sincerely,

Dean Rusk

Dean Rusk

A. Philip Randolph
Educational Fund

260 PARK AVENUE SOUTH / NEW YORK, N.Y. 10010 / (212) 533-8000

April 26, 1982

Ms. Jadie Elliott Hansen
Box 1031
Union City, Tennessee 38261

Dear Jadie Hansen,

I commend your efforts to compile accounts of what various people were doing when they first heard the tragic news that President Kennedy had died.

On that day, I was having lunch at the United Nations, here in New York, with Prince Aga Khan. We were discussing the role of Malcome X in the civil rights movement in America. Naturally, shock and disbelief were the first reaction by everyone present.

I hope the foregoing is helpful to your project, and thank you for thinking of me in this regard.

Good luck on your book.

Sincerely,

Bayard Rustin
President

BR/hrs

MICHAEL RYAN, M.D. *(in 1963) tenth grader in Glendale, California*

I believe the tragedy of the Kennedy assassination is overshadowed by the zealousness of the investigative committee and the millions of tax payers' dollars they are spending. I intend to write my Congressman about it this week!

———

OMAR LOPEZ SANCHEZ *(in 1963) journalist in Venezuela*

JFK's being a Catholic made him a special person, because of the many Catholics in this country. He once went to church with the people when he visited, attended a church near the presidential house. The people mourned his death for days, and there were many memorial services and Masses held in Venezuela. . . . President Kennedy was a friend of our leader, Presidente Romulo Betancourt. I saw JFK at the Maiquetia Airport when he visited there in 1963. There were thousands (probably 20,000 or so) of people lined up to greet him at the airport.

WILLIAM B. SANSOM *(in 1963) senior at The Citadel, The Military College of South Carolina*

I was in my room on Friday afternoon when I heard on the radio that President Kennedy had been shot. Since I was Regimental Commander and reported directly to General Mark Clark, I called him when I heard the news and suggested that he turn on the radio.

After hearing a short time later that the President had died, I called General Clark back and suggested that we cancel the customary Friday afternoon parade and lower all flags on campus to half mast, since many of the Citadel Cadets were visibly shaken by this news. General Clark was reluctant to do this, but after several conversations, all activities for the remainder of the day were canceled.

VINCENT SARDI, JR., *Broadway restaurateur*

SARDI'S

Reservation Phone
(212) 221-8440

EXECUTIVE OFFICE • 234 WEST 44th STREET, NEW YORK, N.Y. 10036 • Tel. (212) 221-8444

October 13, 1980

Mrs. Jodie Elliott Hansen
Box 1031
Union City, Tennessee   38261

Dear Mrs. Hansen:

Like most Americans, I will always remember
where I was when the ammouncement of the attack on
Pearl Harbor was made.

The other indelible moment was when we were
told that President John F. Kennedy had been fatally
wounded. At that time I was in the basement of the
Park Avenue Brick Church making hamburgers for their
Annual School Fair. It was a very joyful and gala
occasion. Suddenly Dr. Wolf called for our attention and announced that President Kennedy had been
shot. Naturally everyone came to a standstill.
At first we were in hopes that it was just a rumor,
but then the radio was turned on and we heard the
actual announcement made. It seems my first in-
stinct was to go home, as it was with everyone else.
I had our English double-decker bus at the Fair
to give the children rides. My family and Margaret
Truman Daniel's children piled into the bus and
I drove everybody home. It was the saddest trip I
ever made in that fun-loving bus.

Sincerely,

Vincent Sardi

VS/rw

PHYLLIS SCHLAFLY

ATTORNEY AT LAW

68 FAIRMOUNT

ALTON, ILLINOIS 62002

TELEPHONE

618 / 462-5415

January 28, 1982

Mrs. Jodie Elliott Hansen
Box 1031
Union City, TN 38261

Dear Mrs. Hansen:

I was attending a Republican Conference at the old Jefferson Hotel in St. Louis when President Kennedy was assassinated. We were shocked at the news and adjourned the meeting immediately.

Sincerely,

Phyllis Schlafly

PETE SEEGER, *American folk singer*

```
                              Box 431
                              Beacon, New York 12508
                              March 8, 1983


Mrs. Jodie Elliott Hansen
Box 1031
Union City, Tennessee 38261

Dear Mrs. Hansen,

     I wish you luck with your book, but I urge that
you get some statements from completely unknown people,
otherwise it will look like just one more autograph
book.

                              Sincerely,


                              Pete Seeger

lb
P.S.  I was on tour in Japan on November 22, 1963.  In
my concert in Tokyo that night, I sang the now famous
song by Ed McCurdy, "Last night I had the strangest dream
I never dreamed before, I dreamed the world had all agreed
to put an end to war."
```

ERICH SEGAL, *author*

Once upon a time I actually saw J.F.K. in the flesh.
Just after he was elected, he came to Harvard for a
meeting of the Board of Overseers. I was there in
the huge crowd surrounding University Hall.

Just before entering the building,   he   turned to
address the ecstatic throng.

"I am here to discuss your grades with President
Pusey. I will defend your interests."

The ensuing roar was indescribable.

On the day he was shot I walked through a very once
empty Harvard Yard to the steps where I had glimpsed
him. I had never gazed upon a human being so <u>alive</u>.

And to this day, I am unable to put my feelings
into words.

RUDOLF   SERKIN

June 14, 1982

Dear Mrs. Hansen,

Thank you for your letter. I think it is an important
project you are working on. I myself clearly and unfor-
gettably remember how I first heard the news of the
assassination of President John F. Kennedy. I was
playing that night at the Teatro Communale in Florence
and during the intermission I was told of that terrible
event. First I felt one should announce it to the audience
and leave silently. But then it was decided to make the
announcement and dedicate the rest of the concert which
was Beethoven's Sonata Appassionata, op. 57 to his memory.
I cannot imagine now how I could have continued to play,
but I did. I hope that this memory will be of some value
to you.

With kind regards and best wishes,

Yours sincerely,

Rudolf Serkin .

LOIS SHANKLIN *(in 1963) resident of Anchorage, Alaska*

My husband worked for Standard Oil and I was at home alone when I heard the news on the radio of John F. Kennedy's assassination. I was very upset and frightened because I thought there was the possibility of another world war. I did not know who Lyndon Johnson was and I was apprehensive about his becoming our President. I called my sister, and she and I stayed together after hearing the news. Our television programs in Anchorage were always about two weeks late, but the news films of the assassination were flown in by the wire services that night—and also the news films of the funeral, etc. were flown in so that we were able to follow the events on television.

WILLIAM V. SHANNON, *U.S. Ambassador to Ireland*, Washington Post *columnist*

EMBASSY OF THE
UNITED STATES OF AMERICA

Dublin, Ireland

July 10, 1980

Mrs. Jodie E. Hansen
Box 1031
Union City, Tennessee 38261

Dear Mrs. Hansen:

I have your letter of June 27 inquiring what I was doing on
the day that President Kennedy was assassinated. I was then
a columnist in Washington for The New York Post. I had lunch
that day at the Statler Hilton Hotel with Frederick Holborn
who was President Kennedy's assistant in charge of correspondence.

As we were passing through the lobby after lunch, we heard and
saw a group of people gathered around a radio at the entrance
to the florist shop. We drew near and in this way heard the
news that the President had been shot and was being rushed to
the hospital. I shall always remember the stricken look on
Fred Holborn's face. He hurried back to the White House and
I to my office in the National Press Building. Shortly after
I reached my office, I had definite confirmation from my news
desk in New York that the President was ~~definitely~~ dead. I
immediately began writing a long memoir for the next day's
paper because I had known him longer and better than any other
member of the Post's staff.

Mrs. Jodie E. Hansen - 2
July 10, 1980

I come originally from Massachusetts and had become acquainted
with him when he was a young member of the House of Representat
in 1950 and I was just starting my career in Washington as a
journalist. Newsmen are so accustomed to responding to events
in terms of what it means for the next edition of the paper and
what it is they must do professionally to get the paper out tha
my only immediate reaction was one of astonishment at the event
"The President" was dead and it was a tremendous story.

Several hours later about nine o'clock in the evening, I was
at home and then my feelings broke through. I realized then

emotionally that "the President" was John Kennedy the
real person I had known, and unexpectedly I burst into
tears.

                              Yours sincerely,

                              William V. Shannon

                              William V. Shannon
                              Ambassador

James William Shore, M.D. *(in 1963) medical school student, University of Tennessee at Memphis*

I noticed that everyone had congregated around the television set in the lobby of the Student Center where I usually played bridge after dining each weekday of school. This action caught my eye, for most of us paid little attention to the television during our lunch break. As I approached the set, I heard repeatedly, "President Kennedy has been shot! President Kennedy has been shot!" Immediately I felt a pang of fear since I suspected that this might be a coup of some kind since our government is now being run by a virtual dictator, the President. However this feeling rapidly subsided as I watched the procedure of inaugurating Lyndon Johnson into the presidency. Shortly thereafter I submerged myself into my afternoon classes and promptly forgot the whole affair, for at that point in my life, being a junior in medical school and trying to finish without problems, I could care less who was President.

William E. Simon
330 South Street
Morristown, New Jersey 07960
(201) 540-9020

November 22, 1983

Mrs. Jodie Elliott Hansen
Box 1031
Union City, TN 38261

Dear Mrs. Hansen:

Many thanks for your October 25 letter. It was only
recently forwarded to me at my current office, hence the delay
in responding.

I remember vividly what + was doing when I heard of President'
Kennedy's assassination. I was having lunch with a friend
at Oscar's Delmonico restaurant in New York. We were
in the middle of a heated discussion about the next day's
Princeton football game when an ashen-faced waiter gave us
the terrible news. The restaurant cleared out in five
minutes fast. I was head of the municipal bond department
at Weeden & Co. at the time, and I walked back to the
office very sadly and somewhat incredulously, and gave
everyone the rest of the afternoon off.

I don't think there's an American alive who was over five
years old in 1963 who doesn't remember exactly what he or
she was doing when they heard the tragic news.

With best regards,

Sincerely,

O. J. SIMPSON ENTERPRISES
11661 SAN VICENTE BLVD.
LOS ANGELES, CALIFORNIA 90049
(213) 820-5702

October 7, 1980

Mrs. Jodie Elliott Hansen
Box 1031
Union City, Tennessee 38261

Dear Mrs. Hansen:

Thank you for asking my impressions and memories of the tragic day President Kennedy died. I will, briefly, try and recount my feelings of that day:

Upon reaching my classroom, I was shocked to see my teacher crying. The announcement of the shooting of President Kennedy was made and the class dismissed.

I felt as though I were in a trance. This was my first encounter with possible death. The bus ride home was completely quiet except for the muffled sounds of crying and sniffling.

How could this happen? Surely the doctors will be able to save his life. How can you kill a President? Heroes don't die -- oh no, President Lincoln.

Thank you again for thinking of me in this regard, and I want to wish you every success with your book.

Sincerely,

O. J. SIMPSON

OJS:cr

CHARLES SKRIPKA, M.D. *(in 1963) second-year medical student in class at Parkland Hospital, Dallas*

I will never forget the traffic, the crowds of people, seeing all the Secret Service men, the political figures, the policemen, the government officials, and the hundreds of curious Dallasites gathered in the parking lot or at the entrance of the hospital. Any well-known politician I had ever read about or seen on the news, it seemed, was there. . . . The atmosphere in Dallas that afternoon and night was a phenomenon like I had never experienced before or since. It seemed as though everything and everyone were functioning in slow-motion.

FRANK G. SLAUGHTER, *author*

May 11,1982

Dear Mrs. Hansen:

As I remember it, I first heard the
last words of a radio broadcast saying President John
Kennedy had been assasinatedted, as I was driving
home from the postoffice.I heard only fragments,so
I hurried home and sat glued to the radio while the
commentator(I believe it was Dan Rather) managed to
keep talking for a long time until the whole series
of climactic events had been described. It was one
of the most dramatic broadcasts I have ever heard
and I sincerely hope not to ever hear one like it ag
again,although the account of Robert Kennedy's assassination rivaled it.And I am convinced that the
shooting of John Kennedy ushered in an era of viol-
lence that will last a long time, until people can
learn the futility ofsolving any problem by violent
means.And having written 60 novelscovering the time
from Joshua's invasion of Canaan to the present, I
can see no likehood of reason prevailing in human rela
tions any time soon. Sincerely,

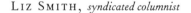

I was having lunch at the Fontana di Trevi restaurant on West 57 Street in New York with my friend, Saint Clair Pugh. Just as we were finishing, a tremor went through the restaurant and people began saying the President had been shot. Saint and I ran out on the street and stopped by a television store where many video screens were all telling us the same thing. It was surrealistic, to say the least. We separated and I returned to my offices in the Allen Funt Productions. Everybody was watching television there in total silence. Then it was announced that the President was dead and many people began to cry. Allen burst out of his private office and said something like, "Well, he's dead. Now all of you get back to work." Nobody answered him. People simply began to collect their things and I think 99 percent of us went home. I went to bed and stayed there for the whole weekend.

Liz Smith
Syndicated Columnist
New York Daily News

October 17, 1979

Mrs. Jodie Elliott Hansen
Box 1031
Union City, Tennessee 38261

Dear Mrs. Hansen:

On the afternoon of November 22, 1963, I
was in the midst of a filming session with
an NBC television crew in my office (NBC
had planned a program on my possible presidential candidacy in 1964) when my Executive
Assistant, Bill Lewis, stepped in and told us
the terrible news about President Kennedy.
We stopped the filming session at once and
Bill canceled all of my public appearance
commitments (the most immediate being the
Air War College, NBC "Today" program, Metro-
media and the Jack Parr program) in deference
to the President.

With respect to my relations with John F. Kennedy,
I would suggest that you get my book "Declaration
of Conscience" (Doubleday 1972) at your nearest
public library. We had not been the best of
friends as he was the only Senator to go into
Maine to seek my defeat (in 1954 the same year
that he refused to support the Democratic candidate against Senator Saltonstall in his own State
of Massachusetts) and he had called me "ignorant"
in 1961 although he sought in 1953 to have me
team up with him on leadership of the New England
Senatorial Delegation.

Ironically enough, shortly before his assassination we had become more friendly. On October 19, 1963 he asked me to accompany him to the University of Maine (on previous Maine visits in violation of custom and tradition of Presidents inviting Senators to accompany them into their states, he had pointedly excluded me from the visiting group on Air Force One) where he was to receive an honorary degree. We talked at length on the flight to and from Washington and Maine and I got to know him better and have a better impression of him. When I returned to the office I said to Bill Lewis, "I think that at last Jack Kennedy is ready to be President!" And at his last press conference, on November 14, 1963, President Kennedy said I would be a "formidable" candidate for president.

His assassination was a shock to me first because he was the President, second because he was a relatively young President, who I felt was ready to improve upon his past record, which I did not think was very good.

Sincerely,

Margaret Chase Smith

BLANCHE E. SOLE *(in 1963) resident of Johannesburg, South Africa*

I had my car radio on and was shocked at the sudden S.O.S. bleep over the air and the announcer came on in a clear but obviously very shaken voice to say, "President John Kennedy of the United States was assassinated in Dallas, Texas, yesterday." There was a two-minute pause and I almost ran into the curb on the side of the road. I was unable to carry on to the beauty shop but turned around and went straight back home to awaken my sleeping family.

ROGER WOLCOTT SPERRY, *neuropsychologist, Nobel Laureate*

CALIFORNIA INSTITUTE OF TECHNOLOGY

PASADENA, CALIFORNIA 91125

April 19, 1982

DIVISION OF BIOLOGY 156-29

Mrs. Jodie Elliott Hansen
Box 1031
Union City, TN 38261

Dear Mrs. Hansen:

Yes, I recall very well that when the news first
reached us I was in the middle of a surgery, clothed in
sterile cap and gown trying to cut some cross connections
between left and right halves of the brain, through a
stereomicroscope, in a test monkey. We continued, of
course, and the patient came through just fine, but from
then on, it was a much subdued and disheartened procedure.

Sincerely,

Roger Sperry

DAVID SPIEGEL, M.D., *physician and cancer researcher*

STANFORD UNIVERSITY MEDICAL CENTER
STANFORD, CALIFORNIA 94305

STANFORD UNIVERSITY SCHOOL OF MEDICINE
Department of Psychiatry and Behavioral Sciences

February 14, 1980

Jodie Elliott Hansen
Box 1031
Union City, Tennessee 38261

Dear Mrs. Hansen,

Thank you for your letter of January 21st inquiring about my memories
of the day when President Kennedy was assassinated for your book.

The event happened at a turning point in my life and marked another one,
I believe, in retrospect. I was a freshman at Yale and remember the
particularly lighthearted manner in which the day started. It was to be
my first experience of the annual Yale-Harvard football game which was to
be played in Newhaven that day. Some friends and I were playing touch
football on the Old Campus, while awaiting the arrival of dates and the
time to go out to the stadium.

I remember someone yelling from a dormitory entrance that President Kennedy
had been shot and at first we thought it was some kind of a joke. Suddenly
portable radios began to appear and we rushed to them to hear the stunned
broadcasters announcing that the President had been shot. I still remember
their initial impression that someone had rushed down the "grassy knoll" and
some ten years later when I visited Dallas for a psychiatric meeting, I
found myself impelled to go to the spot and saw how easy it would have been
for someone to rush over this hill and down to the railroad tracks below.

It was a time when I and my classmates were just experiencing the freedom of
being an undergraduate and the excitement of college life and suddenly it
all changed. The game was postponed for a week and we were all shocked. I
found myself doing something which up to that time had been uncharacteristic,
finding out from friends how I could get on a bus to Washington for the funeral.
It was something I suddenly felt I had to do and I still remember the sight of

Mrs. Kennedy and the leaders of the world marching behind the coffin. It
proved to be the first of many bus trips to Washington, the later one's to
protest the endless war in Vietnam. It seemed as though his death signified
the fact that our government was no longer in good hands and that keeping the
country on a moral track required involvement of the citizens not just the
leaders. Although it was a number of years before I became actively involved
in opposing the war in Vietnam, looking back it seems that President Kennedy's
assassination was a time of particular shock and sadness when I was forced
to look seriously at how the government was being run.

I hope these thoughts will be of use to you.

Sincerely,

David Spiegel, M.D.
Assistant Professor of Psychiatry and
  Behavioral Sciences
Director of Social Psychiatry and Community
  Services, Palo Alto V.A. Medical Center

DS:bm

HARRY KING STANFORD, JR., *president, University of Miami*

STATEMENT FOR MRS. JODIE ELLIOT HANSEN

The first news I received that President Kennedy had been shot in
Dallas came over the intercom system from the pilot of the plane on
which I was returning from Cleveland, Ohio, to Miami, Florida. His
brief announcement was that President Kennedy had been shot, but that
he did not know what his condition was. Everyone on the plane was
benumbed by the news as an awesome silence enveloped the cabin.

My first thought dealt with the irony of this news in contrast
to my mission in Cleveland. I had gone to Cleveland to interview
several persons for the position of Director of the newly-established
Community Relations Board of Dade County, Florida, which had as its
purpose the development of better relations among the ethnic groups
of Dade County. One particular purpose was to give black people and
minority group members an opportunity to have their voices heard concerning any grievances they might have and to have their voices heard
in the development of public policy. The antithesis of my mission to
Cleveland, I thought, was taking place in Dallas.

After a few minutes the pilot came back on the intercom with the announcement that President Kennedy had been shot to death. If possible, the silence even thickened. After the shock of the news began to wane, there was soft discussion among the passengers, no one really knowing the circumstances, but everyone expressing the profound sense of loss and bereavement that he or she felt.

When I returned to campus I found that plans had been made in my absence to go ahead with the football game scheduled between the University of Miami and the University of Florida for the evening of the following day, Saturday. It had been decided to have memorial services at half time for the slain President. The band stood and played three numbers. I gave a brief talk in the Orange Bowl before some 60,000 spectators about the nation's tragedy and about President Kennedy's ideals.

HKS:tr

A L A N S T A N G, *journalist living in New York City, conservative talk radio host*

Alan Stang is a well-known radio personality and an investigative
reporter for American Opinion and Review of the News magazines.
The Alan Stang Report is heard daily on more than one hundred stations and his speeches have been acclaimed throughout the United
States.

In November of 1963 I was living in New York City and was at home

writing a magazine article when I heard the news of the assassina-

tion of President Kennedy. I turned on the radio to the all-news

station and I remember at the time thinking how unusual it was that

they were playing the slow movement of Beethoven's "Eroica." When

the music stopped, the announcement of the President's death was

made. I was shocked and upset, like most Americans, and couldn't

believe such a crime could happen in this country. I stayed at

home the rest of the afternoon and didn't see anyone until I went

out that evening. Everyone I saw was also upset about the news.

I had never met the President and politically speaking, I thought

JFK's administration was collaborating with the revolutionary forces

of that period. One example is my belief that his administration

was responsible for maintaining the dictatorship in Cuba. They lied

to and betrayed the Cuban Freedom fighters at the Bay of Pigs. In

fact, I remember that Robert Welch (the founder and leader of the

John Birch Society) had predicted that they would be betrayed. Our

administration had promised air-cover and on that assurance the free-

dom fighters left Guatemala. They would not have begun that opera-

tion without air cover. Once they set out the air cover was can-

celed.

Back to the assassination, there is no doubt that it was indeed a con-

spiracy. We do not know who or why, but we definitely know it was a

conspiracy---with two or more people involved.

tape-recorded on March 12, 1979

ROGER STAUBACH, *professional football player*

HOLLOWAY-STAUBACH COMPANY 6750 LBJ FREEWAY, SUITE 1100, DALLAS, TEXAS 75240 (214) 385-0500

Roger T. Staubach
PRESIDENT

June 4, 1981

Mrs. Jodie Elliott Hansen
Box 1031
Union City, Tennessee 38261

Dear Mrs. Hansen:

Following are my comments regarding my reaction to President
John Kennedy's death.

I was attending the Naval Academy at the time and was in my dorm
when I heard the news that President Kennedy had been shot. There
was a lot of commotion in the halls and a feeling of total disbelief.
It was later when we went to class that we knew the injuries had been
fatal.

Later, I reported to football practice and we all knelt in prayer.
Of course, we didnot have practice that day, but all stayed around
for awhile, talking about our shock and disbelief of the situation.

President Kennedy was very special to us at the Naval Academy and
since he was such a football fan, we had had the opportunity to
meet him. So this felt even more like a personal loss. We were
scheduled to play Army that weekend, but postponed it for a week
out of respect for the Kennedy family.

Sincerely,

Roger Staubach

RS:rc

ADLAI E. STEVENSON

December 7, 1981

Mrs. Jodie Elliott Hansen
Box 1031
Union City, Tennessee 38261

Dear Mrs. Hansen:

Thanks for your letter of November 18.

I remember well hearing the news that President Kennedy had been shot. I was attending a meeting of a civic organization in Chicago. The news shocked everyone. No one knew quite what to do or say. We didn't, at the time, know he had been assassinated. For lack of anything to do, the meeting continued, though I left to return to my office for more news. It was there that I heard the President had been killed.

I hope this is of some help.

With best wishes,

Sincerely,

SUITE 400   888 SEVENTEENTH STREET N.W.   WASHINGTON, D.C. 20006
SUITE 1955   231 SOUTH LASALLE STREET   CHICAGO, ILLINOIS 60604

JIM STREET, *broadcast reporter*

Full Name _____ Jim Street _____ **Age** 43 _____

Current Address 2408 Catalo, Arlington, TX _____ **Address Nov. '63** El Paso, TX

Occupation or Profession now ___ Public Information Officer - DFW Airport _____
Occupation or Profession Nov. '63 ___ Radio-TV reporter

*Use space below and please include small details, such as: if you saved any newspaper clippings or memorial publications; if you had ever seen or met President Kennedy; if you (at the time) were worried or apprehensive about the possibility of a world crisis or a conspiracy; if your community had any special church or memorial services, etc. **Any small detail is important.***

I was in the newsroom watching the Associated Press newswire. Another newsman was doing a short sports broadcast on the air from the same room. It was during the commercial and his mike was off when the AP machine started dinging, signifying an important story. At the same time, the machine typed out a brief message: "Three shots rang out at President Kennedy's Motorcade in Dallas. No one was hit. The motorcade did not stop."

I turned to my fellow newsman, John Garmon, and said, "Here is something you might want."

Without looking at it, he jokingly replied, "I doubt it."

When he saw the message, he flashed the disc jockey with a light-signal designed to get the disc jockey's attention and waved the bulletin to signify he wanted to air it. As John started to read the information, the machine began ringing again and this time typed simply:

"Kennedy hit. Wounded, perhaps mortally."

I gave the new information to John and he aired it immediately.

Then I dashed down to the television side, ran into the audio booth and, through a headset, told the director to cut into programming and put me on the air. I was out of breath, partially from the run down the hall and partially from excitement over the magnitude of the story I was handling. But I panted the information over the air and gasped to the audience to stay tuned for further details.

It was a few moments before 12 noon (it is an hour earlier in El Paso than Dallas) and I had a live newscast coming up. I discarded the other stories and used whatever I could coming in over the wire. My newscast was part of a 30-minute informal new and interview show but we just did an abbreviated newscast and the station then returned to showing old movies. We were in process of getting network but were not yet hooked up so we had no way of joining the network immediately. We got on before the day was over.

Use back of paper, if more space needed----and for any philosophical comments or historical insight you have, concerning the event.

After that, there was not much to do over the weekend except to gather information for a 30-minute local special we did Monday after the funeral when the network ended its continuous coverage.

DR. PATRICK TAYLOR *(in 1963) student at Memphis State University*

I recall hearing about school children cheering at the news of the President's death. . . . Being a native of Tennessee, I consider myself a Southerner, I did not appreciate once hearing Robert Kennedy say that the South is a "different country." I remember the troops being sent to Ole Miss and the searching of automobiles and confiscation of weapons from private citizens, without martial law. The South got a raw deal, in my opinion, and the Constitution of the United States was being ruined. I voted for JFK, was sorry later, and I was not even close to being as upset as my wife.

The Graduate School and University Center
of the City University of New York

Graduate Program in Comparative Literature
Graduate Center: 33 West 42 Street, New York, N.Y. 10036
212 790-4494

Chesterfield, Mass. 01012
10/13/78

Elliott Enterprises
Tennessee

Gentlemen

Your letter about the projected Kennedy assassination memories,
addressed to the Chesterfield Historical Society, reached me as
its president. In my private capacity--now Adjunct Professor
of Comparative Literature,Graduate School,CUNY, then Professor
of English and Comparative Literature, Graduate School,CUNY and
Professor English,Brooklyn College,NYC--I had a rather unusual
experience of the assassination since I was then abroad. I am
enclosing my own story. I have also begun instigating records
of memories from some of the Society's members. As we are a
very small community in the rural west of Massachusetts and
many of our number have recollections going back a very long
way, some of these might indeed interest you. I trust a few
may reach you.

With good wishes for your enterprise--and the hope that the
contributors will be kept informed about publication,

Yours very truly
Ruth Z. Temple
President, Chesterfield Historical Society

(continued)

My Recollection of the Kennedy Assassination

Nov. 78

Ruth Z. Temple   (aged 69)
Chesterfield, Mass. 01012

My story is probably unique since I was not in the United States
but in France, where I was Fulbright Professor of American Literature
at the University of Strasbourg, living with my friend Geneva Sayre
in Paris near the École Militaire.

We were listening, as we did in the early evening, to the
American news on the Voice of America radio when a program was
interrupted with the brief announcement: "President Kennedy has
been shot in Dallas." As the regular program resumed, and we
waited in consternation and impatience for more enlightenment,
we heard the guns at the École Militaire firing the official
salute to the dead Chief of State. Isolated as we were from
our countrymen, there was noone, we thought, with whom to share
our unbelief and our desolation, but the next morning when we
went out to do our errands we found that the French people were
no less concerned. Our local shopkeepers (who had hitherto,
as is the French way, been polite but distant--never even asking
whether we came from the one place they were sure to know of,
New York) now shook our hands and expressed their condolences
as if we had experienced a personal bereavement. "He was a
wonderful man," they siad, "What will the world do without him!"

We attended the impressive memorial service in the American
Cathedral, massed with flowers and crowded not only with American
officials, civilian and military, from the Ambassador down, but
with, it seemed, every American resident in Paris or passing through,
all obviously in a state of shock. The French Government
organized a memorial service in Notre Dame, and that enormous
Cathedral, celebrating in 1963 its eight hundredth anniversary,
was full to capacity with mourners, French, English, American.

260

DANNY THOMAS *(in 1963) comedian and actor*

When JFK died, an awful lot died with him. I'll never forget hearing the news of the assassination. I was at home with my family in Beverly Hills. I was taping a show that day and was getting ready to leave for the studio. I was in the bathroom shaving when one of my children came running in after hearing it on television. This was my middle child, Theresa (Terri), and she was crying her heart out. What she said then, said it all. Her comment was: "Oh, Daddy, America is old again!" I'll never forget my little girl saying this to me. This was so much insight for a little girl to have, because John Kennedy did make American feel young. He made us feel young and strong. Of course, there had been assassinations and assassination attempts in this country before. I thought this was something in antiquity—something that occurred in the old days of the anarchies—something that was supposed to happen in backward, savagelike countries where there is no real insight or grasp of a democracy. For it to happen in America was more than I could comprehend. To destroy that beautiful man—and for what? What did any-one gain or profit from this brutal crime? I honestly believe that the assassi-nation of JFK was one of the true catalysts that brought about the violence in borderline people, those who were angry anyway. Suddenly they were thinking, "How could they kill that holy innocence?" By their violent acts these people were saying, "If they can do that to John Kennedy, then there is this so-and-so that I don't like, this company, this government, etc. and I can..." People just went wild for the next decade or so; they absolutely went crazy. There were the assassinations of Robert Kennedy, Dr. Martin Luther King.

LEONARD MERRILL THOMAS *(in 1963) ninth-grade music teacher in Brooklyn*

I recall the song the class was singing just before I received the news. It was "Somewhere" from West Side Story *(very popular in the early sixties)—"There's a time for us, somewhere a time for us, hold my hand and we're halfway there, hold my hand and I'll take you there, somehow, someday, somewhere." As the children sang the closing refrain I knew that for JFK the time had come. The children then were told—there too was disbelief and sadness—my sadness was greater. p.s. Our show this year* More About Love *contains the song "Somewhere," and in the sixteen years things haven't changed that much—Have we really learned anything from all the tragic deaths of the sixties?*

VINCENT THOMPSON *(in 1963) teacher at the Tennessee Youth Center in Nashville*

There were about 30 boys between the ages of 16 and 8 there, and 99% were felony convictions. A receptionist came into the classroom and told me the news. Before I made the announcement I remember being somewhat apprehensive about what their reaction might be. They were a tough bunch of boys and I considered the possibility that they might joke or laugh and even be indifferent or nonchalant. They reacted quite the opposite. There was no overt happiness or glee expressed and they were far from being indifferent or untouched by the news. There was a definite atmosphere or aura of extreme sadness in the room.

Looking back, I would compare their reaction to how I think a group of college psychology students probably reacted. They asked many questions about the President and the details or particulars about the shooting. They all seemed to be JFK admirers and supporters. I suppose it was because this President was to them the champion of the underdog, the poor and disadvantaged, and the minority groups. I believe kids like this are the greatest psychologists in the world. Most of them seem to have an innate perceptiveness or gut feeling about people that is quite unique. Their instinctive evaluation of President Kennedy was that he was their President and one who was speaking up for them and sensitive to their feelings—one who considered them to be human beings. They believed he was attempting to help "their type" and the grief and sorrow expressed by them that day was genuine. The news of John Kennedy's death seemed to leave them with a hopeless and despondent feeling.

GRADY F. TOLLISON JR., *attorney*

LAW OFFICES

HOLCOMB, DUNBAR, CONNELL, MERKEL, TOLLISON & KHAYAT

A PROFESSIONAL ASSOCIATION

1127 JACKSON AVENUE

POST OFFICE BOX 578

OXFORD, MISSISSIPPI 38655

601-234-8775

PAT D. HOLCOMB
JACK F. DUNBAR
EDWARD P. CONNELL
CHARLES M. MERKEL
GRADY F. TOLLISON
ROBERT C. KHAYAT
WILLIAM M. CHAFFIN
DAVID T. LAIL
JOHN H. COCKE
JANE M. WILBOURN
MARY ANN CONNELL
RONALD L. ROBERTS

CLARKSDALE OFFICE

152 DELTA AVENUE

POST OFFICE BOX 368

CLARKSDALE, MISSISSIPPI 38614

601-627-2241

January 15, 1979

Mrs. Jodie Elliott Hansen
c/o Hansen Enterprises
Box 1031
Union City, Tennessee 38261

Dear Mrs. Hansen:

In response to your letter of January 6, 1979, I'll be glad
to give you the information requested. I'm afraid the
narrative events will be very brief since it would take a
book to explain my feelings concerning the assassination of
President Kennedy.

My name is Grady F. Tollison, Jr. I am 41. I presently
live in Oxford, Mississippi. In 1963 I lived in Clarksdale,
Mississippi. In 1963 I was a high school football coach and
instructor in American government. Presently I am an attorney.

On the day President Kennedy was assassinated, the girls'
basketball coach was absent. He had asked me to control the
practice for the team in his absence. I was using some football drills, which I knew best, having the girls run backwards.
The star of the team fell and split her head. At about the
same moment, an unexpected cloud came up with torrents of
rain. While I was taking the girl who was bleeding profusely
to the hospital, we heard the news of President Kennedy's
assassination.

Perhaps the most shocking incident was when I returned to the
school and heard a student express glee.

I have been a life-long Democrat and, of course, voted for
President Kennedy in 1960. I cannot tell you the sorrow that
I felt for my country when he was assassinated.

Mrs. Jodie Elliott Hansen
January 15, 1979
Page Two

My personal assessment is that President Kennedy made many
mistakes, perhaps some caused from the exuberance of some of
his youthful advisors; however, I only wish he had been
available to lead us through the '60s. In many respects, I
think his death and the frustrations youth felt as a result
of his death were responsible for the feeling of helplessness
which prevailed among many of our youth in the '60s.

I hope this information is what you requested. I wish
you well with your project.

Cordially,

Grady F. Tollison, J
Grady F. Tollison, Jr.

GFTjr/mg

MALCOLM TOON *(in 1963) diplomat, ambassador to Moscow*

Political Science

MU Marquette University

Milwaukee, WI 53233
414-224-6842/43

December 9, 1982

Mrs. Jodie Elliott Hansen
Box 1031
Union City, Tennessee 38261

Dear Mrs. Hansen:

I apologize for the long delay in responding to your letter of last summer asking for contributions with regard to reminiscences of the day when President John Kennedy was assassinated. I have been busy traveling around the country for speaking engagements, and I am just now getting to the pile of mail which awaited my return.

Perhaps the enclosed contribution may still be of use to you.

Sincerely,

Malcolm Toon

MT/ag
Enclosure

The shocking news of the assassination of President John Kennedy reached me in my apartment in the Embassy compound on Tchaikowsky Boulevard in Moscow where I was posted as Counsellor for Political Affairs in the American Embassy. Other senior officers and I immediately after receipt of the news adjourned to our ninth floor offices in the Embassy in order to prepare for the ceremonies which attend the death of a prominent American public figure at all missions overseas.

We faced two difficult problems. The first--and most sensitive--was the disposition of the file in our consular section on Lee Harvey Oswald. We had heard on the radio that Oswald was the suspected assassin and also that there was some indication of a past tie with the Soviet Union. We knew of course that one of the first questions that would be put to us by the local American correspondents would be with regard to any information that we might have on file concerning Oswald. We felt that we would be best advised to pack up the Oswald file and ship it back to Washington. We would then be in a position to tell the correspondents that we had disposed of the file and therefore were in no position to comment on its contents. Clearly there would be much speculation in the local press corps about a Soviet role in the President's assassination, and it was terribly important for us in the Embassy to avoid any comment which could lend support to such speculation. It was our intention to tell the correspondents that any inquiries with regard to Oswald should be directed to the Department of State in Washington. The Embassy would have nothing to say.

The second problem related to the arrangements for the condolence book which would be open for signature the following day at Spaso House. We discovered that there was no black crepe paper in the Embassy and therefore we had to call upon two of our officers' wives to make available two black evening gowns which we then cut up in order to provide the necessary mourning border for the President's portrait over the book of condolences.

(continued)

The next day a senior official of the Soviet Foreign Office visited the American Embassy--a rare occurrence in Moscow--to inform us that the Prime Minister Nikita Khrushchev who was then on an official visit to the Ukraine would return to Moscow that morning in order to personally sign the book of condolences and thus show his respect for the late President. When Khrushchev arrived several hours later at Spaso House, the Ambassador, then Foy D. Kohler, the Deputy Chief of Mission, Walter J. Stoessel, and I received the Prime Minister and after he had signed the book of condolences he was invited to one of the small salons in Spaso House for coffee and conversation. As we discussed the tragic death of our young President, I noted with amazement that tears welled up in the eyes of Nikita Khrushchev.

I found it difficult to believe that this hard bitten tough old Bolshevik would show such a display of sympathy at the death of the President of the leading country in the capitalist world. It was not as it turned out that Khrushchev was grief stricken over the death of the President; what caused him considerable uneasiness was the fact that he did not know Lyndon B. Johnson who succeeded President Kennedy in the White House and he was a little bit apprehensive as to what sort of policies he would be faced with on the part of the new President. He calmed down and seemed somewhat more comfortable when Ambassador Kohler assured him that the policies which would be followed by the new President would be essentially those which had been followed by the late President Kennedy.

We then settled in to a month of mourning as a tribute to our late President and in a very real sense most of us in the Embassy were not unhappy at the prospect of a month's respite from the wearying social life which characterizes the life of a diplomat in Moscow. I personally was shocked and deeply grieved at the assassination of President Kennedy--not only because I admired him greatly as a young vigorous leader of our country but also because I had known him personally during World War II when we both served as PT-boat skippers in the south and southwest Pacific.

MARGARET TRAUTMAN *(in 1963) housewife in Tulsa, Oklahoma; shortly after the assassination she received this letter from her elderly aunt recalling her husband's burial and the funeral of President William McKinley in 1901*

Dearest Miggie,

The events attending Kennedy's death really left me feeling drained. Everyone identified with what went on, but imagine me, at the end of the burial at Arlington, with my own future grave not far away, and feeling lower than a snake's belly anyway. Having experienced the volley of guns, taps, and the folding and presenting to me of the flag covering Vint's casket, it all seemed too vivid. What a dreadful experience the whole series of events was for all of America.

I was reminded of the funeral of President McKinley in which we had passes which took us to the top of the Capitol steps: My first experience with the sound of the muffled drums, and the Chopin funeral march in slow tempo. It was raining and we looked out over a sea of black umbrellas as the casket was carried up the steps. A gloomy, gloomy scene. And a shock to me to realize how long ago it was, and how vividly I remembered it. By the way, then the Marine band played "Nearer My God to Thee" and I have hated it ever since.

p.s. By the way, the cadence of the Chopin Funeral March *and the muffled drums had been stepped up considerably from sixty years ago. Doubtless the results of the contemporary tempo about everything.*

PAUL J. VANDERWOOD *(in 1963) Peace Corps evaluator on leave from his job as a reporter for a Memphis newspaper*

At the time I was recruiting for the Peace Corps in Philadelphia, and had just arrived at the Statler Hotel. A bellboy asked if I had heard that Kennedy had been shot. I said, "No." He said, "But I guess it isn't serious." I dropped my bags and went to the TV set in the lobby. No news yet on the President's condition. On the way upstairs, the elevator boy said, "Right through the head"—although this had not been confirmed.

Then came the news of his death. I went to my room and cried a lot. I also watched TV. Hours must have passed. I can't remember any details, and I must have been in shock. About 6:00 P.M., I was very numb. What should I do? I decided to go to church—Catholic Church. I am a fallen-away Catholic. I had not been inside a Catholic Church in six or seven years. I went back in this moment of crisis. I haven't been back since. As I wandered along the Philly streets, I remember the gradual appearance of pictures of Kennedy in storefronts, draped in black, and some with flowers. I thought a drink might settle me down, but it didn't. I was morose; I wouldn't talk with anyone. I was grief-stricken.

MORT WALKER, *cartoonist, creator of* Beetle Bailey

 51 Mayo Avenue, Greenwich, Connecticut 06830

May 25, 1982

Dear Mrs. Hansen,

I was bowling with a group of my cartoonist friends when we first heard the news of President Kennedy being shot. Of course we thought it might be a rumor or that he was only wounded so we tried to continue our game. We couldn't. Our hands seemed heavy, our minds were elsewhere. We soon adjourned to a friend's house to watch the tragedy unfold on television through tear-filled eyes.

Good luck with the book. I hope you get a publisher.

Cordially,

Mort

The University of Alabama in Birmingham
Office of Rehabilitation Resources
205/832-3190   ACTS 345-3190

July 9, 1979

Mrs. Jodie Elliott Hansen
Box 1031
Union City, Tennessee 38261

Dear Mrs. Hansen:

In response to your question of what I was doing when I
heard of the assassination of President Kennedy, I was attending a dedication ceremony for a school in Haleyville, Alabama.
I remember that the Sheriff's Department informed us of the
assassination and that Sheriff's Deputies removed me from the
ceremonies because, at that time, they were not sure that it
was not a conspiracy that might involve other public office
holders.

Sincerely,

George C. Wallace
Director

GCW:slo

One Court Square, Suite 219 / Montgomery, Alabama 36104
An Affirmative Action / Equal Opportunity Employer

ELI WALLACH, *actor*

From the desk of ...

ANNE JACKSON
Eli Wallach

Dear Mrs Hansen -

On that fateful day in November - my wife + I were at the Connaught Hotel in London Eng — I was engaged in a film project. The news was brought to us by a distraught Anne Bancroft — who also was a guest at the hotel.

The BBC-TV called + asked if I'd appear on that evening's program to give an American's reaction to the dreadful news — .

The next evening I was asked to read — over BBC-TV part of Pres. Kennedy's inauguration speech. The English also wanted to know if I knew anything

(continued)

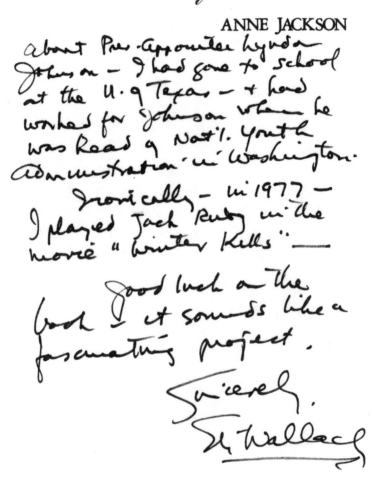

From the desk of...

ANNE JACKSON

about Pres. Appointee Lynda
Johnson — I had gone to school
at the U. of Texas — + had
worked for Johnson when he
was head of Nat'l. Youth
Administration in Washington.

Ironically — in 1977 —
I played Jack Ruby in the
movie "Winter Kills" ——

Good luck on the
book — it sounds like a
fascinating project.

Sincerely,
Eli Wallach

CABLE ADDRESS:
WALLISFILM
LOS ANGELES, CALIF.

TELEPHONE
(213) 273-3381

HAL WALLIS PRODUCTIONS

9200 SUNSET BOULEVARD
LOS ANGELES, CALIFORNIA 90069

May 17, 1982

Mrs. Jodie Elliott Hansen
Box 1031
Union City, Tennessee 38261

Dear Mrs. Hansen:

Thank you for your letter, and, since I have a very clear
recollection of that fateful day, I will attempt to give it to
you briefly.

My son, Brent, and I were having lunch at the Gloucester House
Restaurant on 50th Street in New York City. In mid-lunch our
waiter came to the table and said, "President Kennedy has been
shot." He had no further information as to the severity of the
wound. We quickly paid our bill and made our way to the
Carlyle Hotel where we were staying, turned on the television
set and remained glued to it waiting for bulletins that were
being issued from time to time.

On leaving the restaurant and getting into the maelstrom of
traffic there was a very strange and weird feeling -- with
people rushing along the street, many of them with small radios
held close to their ears, and a pall seemed to hang over the
street and a peculiar silence over it all.

I hope the foregoing is in the nature of what you are after.

Sincerely,

Hal Wallis

HWmrg

MINNESOTA FATS   December 27, 1979

Yes, I remember that day. I was at home in Dowell and just
the day before had been in Dallas, doing an exhibition at the
Bolero Bowling and Billiards Alley. I'm not a TV watcher ---
just happened to have it on that day and heard the news. I
did not get excited. I do not get excited about anything,
understand? I do not react to things like that---like regular people do. I'm not uptight like other people; I keep my
cool. I keep my cool when playing pool and that's why I'm
so good. Anyone like me who has raised himself on the streets
of New York since age 2 --- playing pool for food and cookies
like I did --- does not react to this type of news like the
average citizen. Of course, you understand, when a President
gets killed, any living human will be bothered by it, understand? I knew President Kennedy. I've known all the Kennedys.
I've played pool in the White House lots of times when all the
Presidents were there for years back --- even back to Harding.
I never went to school, didn't have time for it. I was roll-
ing balls around the table since I was 2, and could beat any-
body in sight when I was 8. I hung around taverns, saloons,
pool rooms, etc., 24 hours a day. They used to put me in the
middle of the pool table before I could walk, you understand?
You know, I was supposed to play in the White House with Amy
Carter not long ago --- couldn't make it then, but I'll probably go soon. I'm not political - - - never was . . . .
I've played for presidents, kings, the Pope of Rome, --- and
over the world. Politicians stand in line to hear me speak
and watch my trick shots. I'm a marksman beyond compare;
the world's greatest speaker; and the highest paid entertainer
on earth. You can see Tom Jones 3 times for the price of seeing me just once. People pay more to see me than they pay to
see Frank Sinatra. Yes, I watched TV part of that week-end
when President Kennedy was killed. I was at home here in
Dowell to eat and sleep then, just like I am now, understand?
Yes, nice Christmas --- no big deal, but no little deal either.
You'll see me most anytime you turn on your television. Anheu-
ser Busch just bought me for $6. million. I'll still be trave-
ling around too, understand? The phone rings off the wall . . .
Everybody wants me . . .   .

Minnesota Fats

Rudolf Wanderone

JACK WARNER, JR., *movie executive*

JACK WARNER, JR.
107 North Gunston Drive
Los Angeles, California 90049

March 12, 1981

Mrs. Jodie Elliott Hansen,
Box 1031,
Union City, Tennessee,
38261.

Dear Mrs. Hansen:

Your fascinating letter concerning your project
reached me and I read every word of the enclosures as well
as the letter itself. I was most interested in this collection
you are making of the feelings of other Americans on hearing of
the dreadful event in Dallas. Although it happened so many
years ago... it seems to have occurred only the other day...
so fresh is it in memory and horror.

I do not think I can add much to your assembly of
interesting facts and memories because I was working on a
motion picture production on the day we heard the news on
radio. The picture was never produced... and as it was a
comedy, perhaps it should never have been made in those tragic
times. Perhaps not though... I recall John Kennedy enjoyed a
good laugh and possibly would have said "Go on... make the
damn film! Maybe it will cheer people up..."

I met President Kennedy several times and found him
to be a warm and vital young man. He was the very first
President I ever met who was actually younger than I was...
That kind of impressed me. We first shook hands in a hotel
lobby in Arizona when he was about to announce his candidacy.
I was greatly impressed by his manner, his assurance... and felt
he was a man I could trust and follow. I did that... I worked
for his election and corresponded with him many times... I
recall one very sad letter on the loss of his son when my wife
and I, who had suffered a similar misfortune, wrote the President
and Mrs. Kennedy expressing our sympathy.... and received from
him a wonderful response.... written from his heart. I keep
that letter and others in a special file.

The day of his death.... It was a work day for me...
at a desk trying to make sense out of a senseless scenario for
a comedy. The radio came on... people rushed into the office
and all work ceased. We sat in stunned silence until finally
we heard the last words - that John Kennedy was dead. Many of
us expressed the same thought... A Generation of Americans had
been Robbed! ... This was <u>our</u> President... the first one of
our times and of about our <u>age</u>.... it was as though a little
part of each of us had been assassinated..... That night we
were to go to a friend's birthday party... We went and all of
us sat in silence...still very much in shock.... a shock that is
still with us today.... years later... when so many mediocre men

(continued)

have somehow been allowed to enter the White House. It was
a feeling I had once again some years later when Bobbie Kennedy
was killed right here in Los Angeles. A generation had been
beaten, mugged, raped and robbed once again.... and for it
we received Nixon and Watergate.

These random thoughts have been brought about in
recalling what I am sure was one of the most influencial events
in our recent history. As you noted in your interesting enclosure,
it was almost as though we were living a century ago at the time
President Lincoln was killed... and history was tragically and
decisively altered for us all.

Many thanks for collecting the thoughts of so many
fellow Americans. I am sure it has been a very difficult work
you undertook.... but it is something which is so worthwhile
and will be of such future value that I compliment you on
doing it. May all your efforts meet with good results. I shall
be most interested in hearing what eventually comes of all the
factual and human interest material you have assembled.

With every good wish, I am,

Sincerely yours,

JACK WARNER, JR.

2495 REDDING ROAD
FAIRFIELD, CONNECTICUT 06430

April 16, 1982

Dear Mrs. Hansen:

I have nothing of interest to report.
I was passing the door of our nurse's apartment
(we had small children then) and she stepped out
and told me briefly what she had just heard on the
radio. This is scarcely breath-taking and posterit
ty can no doubt do without the information.

Sincerely,

[signature]

I am a Democrat.

J. D. WATSON, *molecular biologist, Nobel Laureate,*
co-discoverer of the structure of DNA

 Cold Spring Harbor Laboratory
P.O. Box 100, Cold Spring Harbor, New York 11724

March 30, 1983

Mrs. Jodie Elliott Hansen
Box 1031
Union City, Tennessee 38261

Dear Mrs. Hansen:

I was in the Executive Office Building, presiding over a meeting on the Boll Weevil which President Kennedy had asked his Scientific Advisory Committee to look into. The news of the assassination attempt reached us soon after the event and not knowing whether the President was alive we went ahead discussing whether there might be a way to prevent the Boll Weevil entering Arizona from across the border in Mexico. Needless to say, we had no appetite for what we were doing and kept going only through wishing that somehow the President might be able to reassume a meaningful presidency.

When the news that he was dead came, we immediately disbanded and I went upstairs to Mark Raskin's office, where, feeling unbelievably awful and not wanting to talk about the death of our immediate dreams we focused instead on what the new Johnson presidency might mean to the already then bad mess in Viet Nam.

Yours sincerely,

J.D. Watson
Director

JDW/as

William Childs Westmoreland
General, United States Army, Retired
Box 1059
Charleston, South Carolina 29402

April 12, 1981

Dear Mrs. Hansen:

At the time of President John F. Kennedy's assassination, I was commanding the XVIII Airborne Corps of the U. S. Army and Fort Bragg, North Carolina. For the weekend we had as our house guest the Honorable S. Roy the Counsellor General to New York City from India. My wife and I had become friends of the Roy's while I was Superintendent of the U. S. Military Academy at West Point. The assassination of the President was a shock to us all and embarrassing to my wife and I to have such lawlessness displayed to foreign guest in our home.

Sincerely,

W. C. WESTMORELAND

Mrs. Jodie Elliot Hansen
Box 1031
Union City, Tennessee 38261

RICHARD WIDMARK, *actor*

Richard Widmark

April 1, 1981

Dear Mrs. Hansen,

I heard that John
F. Kennedy was shot while
I was working on location
making a movie near
Moab, Utah. It was a
John Ford western called
Cheyenne Autumn. A crew
member was listening to
a transistor radio just as
Ford was lining up a
shot, came running up to
break the news. He imm-
ediately stopped work, Ford
went to his trailer and
asked me to come in. He
was distraught, for he was
a friend of the Kennedy

family and had known Jack
since he was a small boy.
Joe Kennedy had been head
of RKO where Ford had
made among other movies,
the classic THE INFORMER. We
spent the entire afternoon
in the trailer — Ford crying
and wailing — a bit like
an Irish wake. I felt
just terrible, but I think
it helped my distress to
try to comfort Jack Ford.
It was a dreadful day.
I'll never forget it.

Sincerely

Richard Widmark

RICHARD L. WILSON *(in 1963) college student*

My most poignant memory came a day later when the sign was put up on one of the campus cafeteria's door which read:

CLOSED FOR THANKSGIVING

Underneath this printed sign one sorrowful student had written in one color ink:

WHAT HAVE WE GOT TO BE THANKFUL FOR?

And underneath that, another student had written in a different color ink:

THAT HE LIVED.

Tom Wilson, *syndicated cartoonist, creator of* Ziggy

TOM WILSON

Dear Mrs. Hansen,

I was working with my staff of writers and artists in the Hi-Brow Studio at American Greetings Corp. One of the artists had a small portable radio turned on for music. When the announcement came on the tiny portable — everything stopped and total silence came over the room — everyone rushed back in complete disbelief hoping to hear that it was a mistake of some kind.

Every one of us was so stunned that combined with the sobs and distant stares it was evident that no one was capable of creating humor that day — I dismissed the entire staff.

Tom Wilson

We are publishing a book about the memories people have of an unexpected, dramatic, and tragic event in American history. The book will be compiled of personal stories submitted by people of all walks of life, people of all nationalities, and of all political party preferences------telling us where <u>they were</u>, <u>what they were doing</u>, <u>the feelings they had</u>, <u>the reaction of</u> <u>others around them</u>, and <u>how they heard the news</u> of the assassination of the late President John F. Kennedy. The book will <u>not</u> be about his life or his politics. It will be about <u>people</u> and will be one of human interest as well as being historically significant. We have heard from all types of people ------educators, businessmen, lawyers, doctors, housewives, politicians, factory workers, authors, entertainers, etc. We are interested in your story and any small detail you remember will be important and significant.

Received May 5, 1979

Mrs Jodie Elliott Hansen
Box 1031
Union City, Tennessee 38261

Full Name ___Robert C. Young___   Age __64__
Current Address __3601 Porter Street N.W, Washington, D.C. 20016__ Address Nov. '63 __Same__

Occupation or Profession now <u>Correspondent - Chicago Tribune Washington Bureau</u>
Occupation or Profession Nov. '63 <u>White House correspondent -- Chicago Tribune</u>
Use space below and please include small details, such as: if you saved any newspaper clippings or memorial publications; if you had ever seen or met President Kennedy; if you (at the time) were worried or apprehensive about the possibility of a world crisis or a conspiracy; if your community had any special church or memorial services, etc. <u>Any</u> <u>small</u> <u>detail</u> <u>is</u> <u>important</u>.

As a White House correspondent, I knew President Kennedy personally quite well, had met him many times, and saw him frequently in Washington and elsewhere when he was away from the White House. I had no apprehensions or misgivings about his trip to Dallas in November, 1963, although I was aware of the strong anti-Kennedy political sentiments in Dallas, even hostility toward him among certain elements in the city. To me, the Kennedy trip to Texas was a political story, a presidential "peace mission" to try to promote political unity among the diverse and warring factions of the Democratic party in Texas.

On the morning of Nov. 22, I recall listening to a speech Kennedy made to a group in the parking lot of the Fort Worth hotel where he had spent the night. I also recall a Gov. Connally press conference in the hotel and chatting informally with Connally. The White House <u>press contingent from Washington</u> took its place in the Kennedy motorcade from the Dallas airport -- Love Field -- in two chartered buses well to the rear of the procession and out of sight of President Kennedy in his limousine at the head of the motorcade. It was an unseasonably warm

Use back of paper, if more space needed----and for any philosophical comments or historical insight you have, concerning the event.

day and the windows of the bus in which I was riding (I was in the second
of the two White House press buses) were closed because the air conditioning
was turned on. As we rode through downtown Dallas and approached the
point of the assassination en route to the Dallas Trade Mart where Kennedy
was to give a speech at a luncheon of the city's business and civic
establishment, I was preoccupied with my typewriter placed on my lap trying
to finish a story on Kennedy's upcoming speech -- I had an advance copy of
the speech handed out previously by the White House. I was working hard to
finish the story because I was getting close to one of my newspaper's
afternoon deadlines and wanted to file the story with Western Union at the
Trade Mart as soon as we arrived there. I had no time to wait until after
the luncheon and Kennedy's speech to send the story to Chicago. Thus,
in my concentration on writing and because the bus windows were closed,
I was not aware of my surroundings and anything that might have been
happening outside the bus when it came to an abrupt halt near Dealy Plaza.
As was usual whenever a presidential motorcade stopped, the reporters on
the press bus -- myself included -- rushed to the exit door and stepped
outside to see if we could determine why the motorcade stopped. In Dallas
that day, although we were so far back in the motorcade we could not see
very far ahead and the President's limousine was out of our sight, we
presumed the motorcade had stopped either because Kennedy wanted to get
out and shake hands with spectators lining the thoroughfare, or because
of some untoward incident -- such as ~~an overenthusiastic well-wisher, or possibly~~
a hostile spectator or crank breaking through the
police lines and rushing toward the presidential limousine. We figured
it was something to be checked out after we reached the Trade Mart, a
possibly newsworthy incident. But, the last thing any of us reporters
had on our minds was that anything had happened to Kennedy, that he was
even threatened in any way, let alone fatally shot by an assassin. Our
wondering about why the motorcade stopped was pretty much pushed out of our

(continued)

minds when the motorcade started up again -- it had stopped very briefly
so we figured nothing very serious or earthshaking had happened in that
short space of time -- and we had to get back on the bus in a hurry. The
two press buses proceeded on to the Trade Mart as if nothing had happened
and I resumed writing my story. For all we reporters on the bus knew,
Kennedy was still riding in his limousine at the head of the procession.
I can faintly recall that as we �■ rode along, I was aware of people
running in different directions and motorcycle policeman speeding about.
But I want to emphasize, that no one on the press bus had any knowledge or
even any indication at that point that Kennedy had been shot or that anything
serious had happened. What we did not know was that as our bus proceeded
along the scheduled route to the Trade Mart, the limousine bearing the
fatally wounded President was speeding in another direction to Parkland
Hospital. When we arrived at the Trade Mart, our bus took us to the rear
of the building, we got out, and went through the kitchens to the
caverₙous hall where the luncheon was being held and where the guests
were waiting at the tables for the President to appear. I again want to
stress that I and the reporters with me on the bus still did not know
that Kennedy had been shot -- we presumed he had arrived at the Trade
Mart and was in one of the side rooms at a VIP reception prior to entering
the hall to the strains of "Hail to the Chief" and taking his place at the
head table. I can recall clearly riding an escalator to the press room
and Western Union teletype machines on the third floor, my completed story
in my pocket ready to hand over for filing to Chicago, carrying my
portable typewriter. I recall chatting, making small talk with ● a
fellow reporter -- Carleton Kent (now retired) of the Chicago Sun-Times --
commenting on the modernistic decor of the Trade Mart as we made the slow
and leisurely ascent on the escalator, still ▂▂▂ unaware ▂▂▂
anything was wrong, that the President was at that ▂ moment in a hospital

some ~~close~~ distance away near ~~⬛~~ death. We did not know Kennedy had been shot until perhaps a couple minutes later when we arrived in the press room and a White House radio reporter shouted out the news of the assassination after hearing it by telephone from his Dallas station affiliate. It was not until perhaps a year or two later that I learned from the White House transportation official on duty in Dallas that day that we might have learned of the assassination sooner had it not been for a curious turn of events. It seems that the driver of our press bus took a wrong turn at the Trade Mart and instead of taking us to the front entrance, deposited us reporters at the rear entrance --hence our making our way to the main hall through the kitchen. We didn't know the difference --we assumed that's where we were ~~supposedly~~ supposed to be let out of the bus. If we had arrived at the front entrance as scheduled, we would have noticed immediately that Kennedy's limousine was not there and thus been tipped off that something was ~~⬛~~ wrong. As soon as we learned the ~~⬛~~ President had been shot, we raced from the press room, down the escalator, back through the kitchen and into the press bus parked ~~⬛~~ in the rear. We proceeded at breakneck speed to the hospital and a scene of incredible confusion. In time, the White House set up a press room in a vacant nurses' classroom and before long, came the announcement that the President was dead, the victim of the rifle bullets of an assassin. In time and with ~~⬛~~ persistence and luck, I found a telephone in a hospital office and was able to get a line through to Chicago. I dictated my story to the Chicago Tribune.

As to my personal reactions and state of mind: The President's assassination was so cataclysmic, so stunning, of such enormity, that I could scarcely believe it had happened and my ~~⬛~~ emotions could not assimilate ~~⬛~~ it immediately. ~~It was all too sudden to grasp right away. The unthinkable had happened.~~ From a professional and journalistic standpoint, this was all to the good because in this numbed and detached

(continued)

state, I was cool and calm and thus better able to deal with the story

I had to handle -- by far the biggest and most earth-shaking story before

or since in my long career in the newspaper business (I am retiring from

the Chicago Tribune Sept. 1 of this year after nearly 40 years on the

newspaper and 43 years in the news business). In other words, the ~~whole~~ event

~~was too traumatic, too incredible to,~~

of the assassination ~~didn't~~ immediately sink in -- I simply couldn't

~~or accept the enormity of~~

recognize what had happened as far as my emotions were concerned, although

mentally I was functioning as a reporter covering an event. This state

continued for several hours --through the dash in the press bus ~~~~~~~~~~~~~

from the hospital to Love Field to cover the swearing in of Lyndon Johnson

aboard Air Force One before his take-off with Kennedy's blood-stained

widow for Washington, through my return to the press room of the Trade

Mart to sit down at my typewriter and write an updated and more complete

story to send to Chicago. I spent the night in Dallas and returned to

early the next morning,

Washington to plunge immediately into covering the new Johnson

administration, the ~~~~ swiftly-flowing events at the White House as

Johnson took over, and then the Kennedy funeral.

May 3, 1979.

/// ////

Robert C. Young
Chicago Tribune
1707 H Street N.W.
Washington, D.C. 20006

E. R. ZUMWALT, JR.
ADMIRAL, U. S. NAVY (RET.)

3 June 1981

Mrs. Jodie Elliott Hansen
Box 1031
Union City, Tennessee 38261

Dear Mrs. Hansen:

At the moment that I learned of the assassination of President
Kennedy, I was in the office of the Honorable Paul Nitze, Assistant Secretary of Defense for International Security Affairs.
I was working for him as a Captain in the Navy, filling the
position of Director of Arms Control. We were having an intense
discussion concerning how best to carry out the arms control
policies of President Kennedy when Paul Nitze's secretary,
Margaret Martin, rushed into the room to report that the President had been shot.

We spent the rest of the afternoon in a state of shock, watching the subsequent tragedy portrayed on television.

Sincerely,

E. R. Zumwalt, Jr.

1500 Wilson Boulevard
Arlington, Virginia 22209
703/841-8960

ACKNOWLEDGMENTS

First and foremost, we thank the hundreds of people who responded to Jodie's query and led her to others. We regret we could not publish them all. Then, we are grateful to those who helped us bring this book to fruition.

Our family: Fritz Hansen, Jodie's husband and Laura's dad, whose patience with this and our other pursuits is legendary. Jim Stubbs, Laura's husband, who gave us the time, space, and encouragement to work as a team. Laura's sisters and their spouses, Lisa and Dr. Rob Ray, and Poppy and Cliff Beach; Laura's brother, Rick Hansen. Betty and Duke Johnson, Jodie's sister-in-law and brother-in-law; and Jodie's brothers and their spouses: Jerry and Carolyn Elliott, Stewart and Nell Elliott, Dr. Barney Elliott and Carolyn Elliott, and Dr. Robert Elliott and B.J. Elliott—as rock solid a support network as you will ever find.

Our agent, Loretta Barrett, who immediately grasped what Jodie and her project were about; and Bettina Schrewe for getting us to Loretta. Our publisher and editor, Thomas Dunne, who was enthusiastic from the first (and he knew who Gorgeous George was).

Reed Massengill, for his wise creative counsel fifteen years ago; and Rosten Woo, whose advice this time around gave us the momentum we needed.

Jodie reserves special appreciation for Danny Thomas. He gave her credibility and the confidence to aim high.

Union City, Tennessee, friends: Judge Bill Acree and family; Stockton and Jenny Adkins; Jere and Nancy Baldridge; Dr. Bob Clendenin and Martha Clendenin; The David Critchlow family, Mary Jewel Critchlow; The Union City Daily Messenger; Butch and Debra Dellinger; Jere and Sacchi Doss; Charles and Betty Dunn; Keith and Anita Fisher; Newell and Betty Graham; Senator Milton Hamilton and Dale Hamilton; Dr. Joe Harpole and Mary Lou Harpole; Jim and Ann Hibbler; Billy Bob and Shirley Kaler; Hunter Kirkland; Robert and Jenny Kirkland; Dr. David Parks; Marian Parks; Jim and Martha Rippy; Ann Stowers; U.S. Representative John Tanner and Betty Tanner; Judy Jernigan Taylor; Bob and Patti Thomas; Melissa Christian Uniao; Tom and Pat Wade; Barry and Lois White; Phillip and Elizabeth White; and Dr. Bobby Young and Cheryl Young. A special thank-you to Patsy Bruff and Joan Ransom for the recent calls; and for the enthusiasm of the Union City Post Office clerks.

Knoxville, Tennessee, friends: Jean Anglin; Todd Wright

Nashville, Tennessee, friends: Nancy Dunn; Al and Ruth Starr Strayhorn; and David Vaughn.

Lexington, Kentucky, friends: Don and Helen Mills.

Sebring, Florida, friends: Jack and Joyce Bachtel; Fred and Mary Meyers.

Billings, Montana, friends: Dr. Kedric H. Cecil; Lainie Fitzpatrick

Morristown, Tennessee, friends: Jack and Nancy Fishman and Michael Fishman, publisher, *The Citizen Tribune*; John Gullion; managing editor, *The Citizen Tribune*.

The following people were very helpful in typing, research, and contacts: Autumn Trace neighbors; bridge club friends; Betsey Brock; Jean Carter; Doris Chapman; Sharon Hipshire; Betty Miller; Kathy Mullins; Wanda Neal; Beverly Quillen; Jean Rich; Donna Simpson; and Charlotte Tolliver. A special thanks to Gayle Bruce, for her wisdom and her above-and-beyond enthusiasm.

The archivists, journalists, and public officials who generously provided background information on the day President Kennedy was killed: Tom Wicker of *The New York Times*; Robert C. Young of the *Chicago Tribune*; Rudy Maxa of *The Washington Post Magazine*; Jack Gertz and other AT&T officials; The New York Stock Exchange; U.S. Military Academy at West Point; U.S. Air Force Academy; U.S. Naval Academy; The Citadel; Andrews Air Force Base; the Vatican; BBC; and the Billy Graham Evangelistic Association.

Laura's friends and colleagues, who provided feedback and contacts: Stacy Abramson; Yazmany Arboleda; Jenifer Berman; Betsy Bradley; Torben Brooks; Leanne Burney; Curtis Cravens; Jenny Douglas; Katherine Eban; Penny Falk; Jim Fields; Steve Fishman; Robin Freidman; Salome Galib; Steve Godeke; Dana Goldberg; Liz Greenstein; Ilana Harlow; Dave Isay; Jodi Kantor; Pamela Clarke Keogh; Ken Lustbader; Jane McNamara; Chris Neville; John Oddy; Kaari Pitkin; Ted Porter; Marci Reaven; Melanie Rehak; Damon Rich; Sherri Schottlaender; Naomi Seixas; Peter Sistrom; Bethany Wall; Suzanne Wasserman; Vicki Weiner; and Steve Zeitlin.